Dod, may God strengthen y...

~~~~~ ~~~~~ 2 0...

S0-BCN-329

SONGS FROM THE PIT

STEVEN MASSEY

SONGS FROM THE PIT

STEVEN MASSEY

Paley, Whately ⊕ Greenleaf Press

Songs From the Pit

by Steven Massey

Copyright 2017, All Rights Reserved

Illustrations by Philip Frusti

Cover by Julius Broqueza

Website: www.SongsFromThePit.com

Published by Paley, Whately, and Greenleaf Press

An imprint of the Athanatos Publishing Group

www.athanatosministries.org

ISBN: 978-1-936830-98-5

Dedicated to:
Jill, my wife, who I love and miss every day.
Marco, my son, who walks with me and makes me smile.
My God, who has wiped away the tears, held me in his arms, and strengthened me through the grief.

Table of Contents

*Note: page numbers reflect the page the devotional reflection be-gins. The corresponding poem and Scripture reading will immediately **precede** the devotional reflection.*

Songs from the Pit

As I read different Psalms, I saw the image of the pit to describe a time of great personal difficulty. When the idea of this book came to me, I felt like I was in a pit with no escape from so many destructive emotions. I thought "what better way to describe my grief walk?!" So the title of the book was born.

As you will see in the poem, "Walking into the Canyon", there are phases that speak to the descent into and out of the pit. Now I know technically, one cannot hike in and out of a pit. But the imagery is powerful, and it describes beautifully the desperation one feels when overwhelmed by grief and depression. Poem 1 describes some of the steps in my grief journey. In this book, poems 2-16 describe my descent into the pit. The bottom of the pit only has two poems. After all, once somebody reaches the bottom, one does not want to linger there. Poems 19-27 address the time of healing. There is still a lot of pain while one heals, as one climbs out of the canyon, but one look ups and sees that progress is being made slowly and steadily climbing out of the pit.

Psalm 40

I waited patiently for the LORD;
he inclined to me and heard my cry.
He drew me up from the pit of destruction, out of the miry bog,
and set my feet upon a rock, making my steps secure.
He put a new song in my mouth, a song of praise to our God.
Many will see and fear, and put their trust in the LORD.

Acknowledgements

This book begins with a thank you to a couple that I never met. When I was nearly two years old, Vernon and Marilyn Wedell gave birth to Jill Rene. She was the first of three children born to this couple, who raised her in the fear and the love of God. Her siblings, Heidi and Thomas, helped shape her to be the wonderful person that she grew to be. I am thankful for this family in which Jill was raised.

I am thankful for Yvette Seltz, who played matchmaker. Without her introducing us and encouraging me to contact Jill, there would be no story. Also, without her coaching Jill about me, there would be no story.

I must say a big thank you to the people of St. Paul Lutheran, Phoenix, Arizona. They were very supportive before and after my wife's passing. They not only welcomed me and Jill; they also welcomed Marco. God could not have given me a more understanding and loving congregation. Thanks especially to the Quiñones and the Ahrens, who helped with Marco whenever I needed help. I apologize for the many good friends that I fail to mention by name, but you are in my heart.

I also need to mention the wonderful family into which I was born. I am the fourth of five children born to Wilbur and Mary Massey. I thank God so much for this couple who raised me. I also thank God for each of my siblings - Bill, Jeff, Diane, and Brad. I am so grateful for the additions that came into the family through marriage- Gayle, Nita, Bob, and Alaine, and their children, my nieces and nephews. I know that you will always be there for me.

To the members of St. John's Lutheran Church of St. Johns, Michigan, I thank you for your words of encouragement and your support through one of the most difficult times of my life.

There is a special friend who walked with me and encouraged me through my grief journey, and especially this last year and a half. Her name is Cher Sproul. I could not have asked for a dearer and more patient friend. She called at the right time and helped walk me through the darkest times. I don't know where I would be today without her encouragement, her counsel, her support, and her prayers. I pray that everyone who reads this has a friend like Cher. She has been God's messenger of hope.

I am grateful for all of you who have prayed for me throughout these years. It has not been an easy journey, as these poems will make obvious. But I know that I am able to be a witness to the goodness of God because of His faithfulness and the faithfulness of God's people, who bring the broken and the hurt before the throne of the God of grace.

A big thank you goes out to my friends who helped clean up my messed up thoughts and bad grammar. Thank you, Rev. Dr. Eric Moeller, Lori Looker, Rev. Jeff Sippy.

Finally, I want to thank God for the precious boy with whom I have walked this road. Marco has given me purpose in life and a focus to go forward in joy and hope. Through this time, he has given me a reason to begin and end the day. During the day, his smile and his zeal for life have given me a reason to smile and to hope that we will wake up to a day in which realizes Jesus' promise- "I came that they may have life and have it abundantly." John 10:10

About the author

I was born and raised in the state of Michigan. My dad was a state trooper for Michigan State police. That meant we moved around Michigan every 5-7 years. If you are interested I can show you where Reed City, Battle Creek, Waterford Township, and St. Johns are on my portable Michigan map.

Upon graduation from St. Johns High School (1978), I began my college life at Concordia College, Ann Arbor (1978-1982). Here I studied to become a Lutheran pastor. I then took a year off from academia and served as a Youth Staffer (a voluntary youth worker) for the Nebraska District of the Lutheran Church Missouri Synod. This was followed by my seminary studies at Concordia Seminary, St. Louis (1983-1988). Part of my studies was a two year vicarage in Zacapa, Guatemala. It was a life forming and transforming experience.

I have often joked, "join the church; see the world." During my years of ministry, I have served as Missionary at large to the Hispanic community in Detroit and other places in Michigan. I have served as pastor in East Peoria, Illinois, Manhattan, New York, Chicago, Illinois, Phoenix, Arizona, and St. Johns, Michigan. I was also a missionary in Jamaica, West Indies, and part time teacher in Maspeth, Queens and Chicago. Presently, I am serving as a Hospice chaplain.

It was Yvette Seltz who introduced Jill to me. I had the role of tourist guide to her single lady friends. I must have been tour guide dozens of times. The only thing that I remember about many of the tours that I gave was a perplexing question. "Why does Yvette need me to be tour guide? She knows the City as well as I do." I never figured what she was up to until later. I was oblivious. Less than a month before I was heading to Chicago, I met Jill. She was an accomplished lady, having moved up the corporate ladder in the telephone industry to the level of middle management. She had traveled internationally. I ate sushi the first time because of her. She treated me the musical "Fosse" when she came to Chicago the first time. She introduced me to Drambuie. Sorry, I am getting ahead of myself. The Lord was opening a whole new life to me through this woman. Now back to New York.

The day we met, I had preached at a church in Brooklyn and raced over to Church for All Nations, not far from Columbus Circle. I performed my tour guide duties. The evening ended with my first taste of sushi. There was something about her that I liked but our lives were going in opposite directions. She was up for a promotion with AT&T in Tampa and I was heading to Chicago.

After a year in Chicago, I called Yvette to catch up, and the topic of my loneliness came up. I made the mistake of telling her that I never had the opportunity to meet anybody. Yvette exploded. She started to name off all the single ladies for whom I played "tour guide." As she rattled off the names I thought to myself, "Oh, that's what she was doing." After about twenty names, she mentioned Jill. I told her that Jill had made a good impression. So after nearly a year since we met, I contacted her. It should be added that during that year in Chicago, I had zero contact with her. It just happened that Jill was coming to visit her Aunt Elly and Uncle Marv, who live in a northern suburb of Chicago. A month later we got together. In the meantime, Yvette was working behind the scenes unbeknownst to me. She told Jill that if she wanted things to develop between the two of us, she would have to make the first move. So during the visit, she kissed me and the romance begun. Most of our courtship was long distance. We emailed each other daily and instant messaged at least once a week. By Valentine's Day, we were engaged. In July, we were married. It was the year 2000. I joked that I would always know how many years I was married. It was the perfect plan.

In our life together in Chicago, Jill worked at Lucent Technology. Due to my ability to speak Spanish, I served the Evangelical Lutheran Church of Dr. Martin Luther, a Slovak church on the south side in the predominantly Spanish speaking community of Gage Park. Jill was a very loving and supportive wife. She was not a person who liked to have the spotlight. She did all the things that were my shortcoming. A perfect example of this was our English as Second Language ministry. I was the one who was up in front. I welcomed and interacted with the students who would come in. Jill did all the paperwork and administration. She also watched the children of the students who came. Jill was a wonderful help. She also encouraged me in what was important to me. This is best demonstrated by her becoming a part of The Servant's Heart ministry, a mission agency working in Guatemala City, Guatemala. She was everything that I needed. But more importantly, she was the one I loved and who loved me.

After five years in Chicago, we received and accepted a call to St. Paul, Phoenix, Arizona. Again, we lived in a predominantly Spanish speaking community. Again, Jill was my support in ministry. It was here though that we began to pursue expanding our family. Since we were not able to have children, we looked at adoption. We opted for international adoption from Guatemala due to our history with this country. Filling out all the paperwork became her "part-time job". We were so excited when we heard that we were accepted and that a baby boy would be our son. We took two trips to Guatemala. On the first trip, we met our son and his foster mother. On the second trip, we brought Marco home. Jill's life was now complete. She was a mother.

Jill was a wonderful mother. She poured her heart and soul into raising our boy. Marco was blessed to have such a devoted mom. He was born a month premature and he has some lasting delays. All his benchmarks were late. He did not start to walk until he was nearly two. He did not start to talk until he was nearly four. Jill did the paperwork to make sure he received the therapy that he needed. She drove him all around the Phoenix area taking him to therapy. I cannot imagine ourselves being any happier than we were.

In spite of our happy life, it was not perfect. Jill had some rheumatoid arthritis. This brought with it medical issues. As a result of the disease and some pretty strong medication, she was hindered from doing some of the things that previously we did together, such as hiking. She did not let this get in the way of our life together. I'm sure she was struggling much more than she was letting me know.

History of my Grief Journey

The happiness of our wonderful life; the joy of our ministry all changed in a tragic moment. It was a Sunday evening. That morning we went to church. In the afternoon, we relaxed with margaritas, using limes from our Mexican lime tree in the backyard. That evening, Jill started complaining of a headache. That was not unusual; she would get migraines. But this one was different. When I supported her as she walked towards the bathroom, she collapsed. Not another word was spoken. After I called 911 and the paramedics took Jill to the hospital, I tried to leave Marco with friends, but everybody was sound asleep. So Marco went with me to the first hospital, where we were informed that she had blood on her brain and was being taken by helicopter to another hospital on the other side of Phoenix. Marco went with me to the second hospital. On the way over to the second hospital, I stopped by a friend's house to see if they could be roused from sleep. No response. So we drove to the hospital where we spent a sleepless night together in the hospital only knowing that our life would never be the same. To be honest, I do not remember many details. I knew our life would never be the same but I had no idea to what extent. I tried to get Marco to sleep but things were different and he was all wound up. Marco asked over and over again what was wrong with mommy and how she was doing. All I could tell him was that the doctors were trying to help mommy.

Around 6 A.M, the doctor came to tell us what was happening. They were words that changed everything and tore apart my life. "Your wife is brain dead. The artery at the base of her skull erupted. There was nothing that could be done." Just like that, in an instant, everything changed. One instant, Jill was with Marco and me; the next she was gone. She was with our Lord.

In the days and weeks that followed, I tried to keep life as normal for Marco as was possible, considering our loss. I tried to carry on. I am so thankful that Jill's sister and niece, Heidi and Kristi, came so quickly and spent the next days with us. Heidi helped me with funeral arrangements and details that needed to be addressed with a clear mind. Kristi helped keep Marco entertained. My family also came quickly and helped me. To be honest, I don't have a lot of memories of that time, only that they were there. I just know that for a while, my home was not a place of comfort. It was where my wife died, and I didn't want to be there by myself.

For Marco's sake, life continued. All we had known- any sense of normal- was gone. Every day was a reminder that my wife was no longer with us. It took me over a month to sleep in our bedroom again. Just walking through the room on the way to the bathroom was a reminder that this is where Jill left us. Marco was my salvation during this time. I poured my life into keeping my son happy. We did the things that made him happy. We walked along the golf course waiting to see the sprinklers. We ate out at the restaurants of West Gate to watch Water Dance, the musical fountain. I did whatever I could do to keep Marco happy. Marco was such a happy child. I wanted him to stay that way. In retrospect, I did not honor all that we lost when Jill died. But I succeeded in my goal. He was happy.

I kept myself strong by living my faith and showing all that I believed in the resurrection. I told myself that if I stayed home, I would drive myself crazy. So after a couple of weeks, I returned to my role as pastor. I lived out my loss in front of the whole congregation by preaching during the final Sundays of Easter. Each Sunday was a proclamation of Jesus' victory over death. I was an inspiration to those who knew my story. But I failed to grieve. I was a testament of one who believed what he preached. But I failed to grieve. I let my grief be hijacked by taking care of everybody but myself. I did not realize this until it was too late.

As I reflect on what I just told you, I hope that I did not give a false impression. I said that I did not grieve. That does not mean that I did not mourn. Many nights I cried myself to sleep. My heart was ripped out when Jill left us. Eight hours of sleep a night became a rarity. Marco mourned as well, but in a different way. He repeated what he knew over and over again. "Mommy died. Her brain broke. She's with Jesus in heaven." I let Marco and myself feel the loss, but I failed to embrace it. I wanted to keep Marco happy and I wanted to keep the faith.

This failure to grieve became apparent after I returned to Michigan as the Associate Pastor at St. John's Lutheran Church. With the move, I lost whatever sense of stability I had. We had a home, which was the only home Marco knew up to that point. I had a congregation that I served for nine years and some very dear friends. I was the pastor and I knew what I had to do. Everything was different when we moved. Mentally, I shut down. I was unable to make the simplest decisions and perform the basic functions of my calling. I was unable to think and come up with creative ideas. When we brain stormed, I had nothing. Sleep deprivation took over. Four hours of sleep was all I would get, even if I took a sleeping pill. The reality was that I was a sinking ship and my ministry was not going to end well. The Senior Pastor, who was a high school and college friend, encouraged me to be the pastor he knew me to be, but nothing worked. He encouraged me to see a counselor. He encouraged me to get a sleeping test, because sleep deprivation was taking its toll on me. The stress and the complicated grief held me captive and I was not functioning to my abilities or the abilities that the church expected of me. After nearly a year, I resigned as pastor of the church. I needed to get better.

The next five months after my resignation were a nightmare. What little stability I had before was no longer there. I had always identified myself as a pastor. There were things that I did every week that gave my life order. It was gone. I had lost my wife, now I lost my calling. In the process, I lost love and respect for myself as well. The only thing that kept me going was to keep life as normal as possible for my son.

Yes, I was finally dealing with my grief. Now there were other losses that I had to deal with. Who was I? I was unemployed. My finances were drying up. I had no structure to order my day. I had lost what support I had from being a pastor. My day was spent with the thought that I had failed in almost every aspect of my life. I was a failure as a pastor. I was a failure as a provider for my son. I was a failure in taking care of myself. Those were the thoughts that plagued me by day and by night.

I started to see a counselor, which for me was huge. Although I was hurting, I did not let people know. For the most part, I kept it to myself. This was a big part of the problem. Not only did I keep things to myself, I isolated myself from people who would have been willing to help. For that reason, the members of the church were surprised when I resigned. Seeing a counselor allowed me to voice what was going on in my life and to have an objective voice react and lead me through the pain and the emotions.

I took my son to Ele's Place, an agency for children who have lost a significant person in their life. While there, I was part of a support group for other parents in a similar situation. Again, it gave me a chance to talk about the loss of Jill in an open and understanding atmosphere. Everyone in the group had lost a spouse and had children to care for during this time.

One of the best things that I did during that time was go to a retreat center for church workers who were beat up in ministry, Shepherd's Canyon Retreat, Standing Stone. One of the benefits was that I was able to deal with my pain and my emotions without having to think about Marco. He was having a great time in Phoenix with his friends. While there, the old me started to come back. I was making jokes. I was laughing and making people laugh. I was able to start reflecting on where I was and what got me to this point. It was there that I wrote the song, "Standing Stone." The writing of that song helped the cleansing and healing to begin. God used that time to get me back on the right path. My nephew, Brian Massey recorded it and sent it to me on my cell phone. I spent many times hitting the replay button. The healing continued and continues.

But grief is an up and down battle. After I returned from Arizona, I started to feel better. I felt that the worse was behind me. I was seeing a counselor. I was sleeping better. I started to enjoy life again. The trigger that started the downhill turn was a visit with a couple pastor friends. They helped me rehash the four months of the new year up to that point. After that I realized that I had not grieved this loss in my life. Soon sleep deprivation came back. Four hour sleeps again were the norm. My mind was racing during the night. I focused on my funds getting low. My financial obligations increased. Now I had to pay my health insurance. I felt abandoned by my church and the leaders who were supposed to look after the workers. One Saturday night, it started to come crashing down. I'm sure I was on the verge of a breakdown. I woke up in the middle of the night and felt numb. I looked in the mirror and wondered who I saw. I went to church but I was not myself. I did not hide my sadness and people noticed. I came home not feeling any consolation from the message that I heard. I needed to pour myself out to the Lord. I prayed that day as I walked around my yard, "Lord, you can't take much more. I'm just a man. Help me."

I had another sleepless night, but this night was different. When I couldn't sleep, I said to myself. "If You won't let me sleep, I'm going to take advantage of this time." I started to write down titles for poems. Most of the titles came within a couple weeks of that low point. I wanted to give a voice to my grief and for others who are grieving. I wanted Jill's memory to be honored, not the source of my fall. In our life together, Jill was with me and supported me every step of the way. Jill brought Marco into our life. Jill managed the house and let me deal with ministry while she dealt with life. In my descent into grief and depression, the loss of Jill was defining me. I did not want the one who brought so much joy into my life to be seen as the one who is seen as the cause of my downfall. In life, Jill held me up and was the love of my life. I hope that the memory of that love will continue to be a source of strength.

Within a couple of days of praying to God, a full time position as a hospice chaplain in Lansing, Michigan became available. Marco and I would not have to move. I had looked for this for months. In the Lord's timing, this all started to happen.

My grief journey is three years and counting. I'm just now starting to get back on track. I believe I went through this so that I could give grief a voice for many who are struggling with grief from whatever source.

For whatever reason you are reading this book, I pray that you have an experience with the living God, who created us. He gave His life for us and gives us life. He lives in us so we can live with Him. If you are grieving, I pray this helps you as you walk that dark and painful road. I especially pray that you will wake up one day and celebrate that this is the day the Lord has made and will rejoice and be glad in it. Be assured of this; you are not alone as you grieve.

Standing Stone

This is the song that began the healing process. It is also the song that best describes the different stages in my grief. There are four stones that are mentioned in this prayer. The significance of each stone will be discussed. You will notice that each verse ends with "Halleluiah". Although it is the same word, it signifies something different each time. I will combine verses two and three into one discussion. These are the pit verses, at the bottom and beginning to come out.

Standing Stone

I come before this Standing Stone
Full of sorrow and all alone,
As a broken child, I'm calling out to ya.
The stone reminds me of deeds you've done.
The battles fought, the vict'ries won
For all to see is written Alleluia.
Alleluia! Alleluia! Alleluia! Alleluia.

I come to you with pain and fear
Struggling through this vale of tears
With just enough strength to cry out to ya.
But sadness is my one refrain.
A broken life is what remains.
Will there ever be another Alleluia?
(Hum)

You come to me in my brokenness
You recognize my pain and stress.
You whisper in my ear, "I am with ya."
You hold me in your warm embrace,
Gently wipe tears from my face
Assuring me you are my Alleluia.
Alleluia! Alleluia! Alleluia! Alleluia.

I come now to your burial tomb,
With no hope and full of gloom
I'm so saddened by what my sin did to ya.
The stone's been moved. The body's gone.
Death is dead. The vict'ry's won.
All is changed there's only alleluia.
Alleluia! Alleluia! Alleluia! Alleluia.

I come to you my cornerstone
Though you stand I struggle on.
At times it's so hard to just hang on to ya.
Yet you show up and you are near.
You speak to me, remove my fear
Calm comes back you restore my alleluia.
Alleluia! Alleluia! Alleluia! Alleluia.

One day I'll stand before your throne.
When everything will be made known.
Those blazing eyes will be looking right through me.
The hand that wiped my tears away
Opened the door for me to stay,
Will give a stone with my new name "Alleluia".
Alleluia, Alleluia, Alleluia, Alleluia!

Scripture Readings for Day 1:

1 Samuel 7:5-12

Then Samuel said, "Gather all Israel at Mizpah, and I will pray to the Lord for you."

So they gathered at Mizpah and drew water and poured it out before the Lord and fasted on that day and said there, "We have sinned against the Lord." And Samuel judged the people of Israel at Mizpah.

Now when the Philistines heard that the people of Israel had gathered at Mizpah, the lords of the Philistines went up against Israel. And when the people of Israel heard of it, they were afraid of the Philistines.

And the people of Israel said to Samuel, "Do not cease to cry out to the Lord our God for us, that he may save us from the hand of the Philistines."

So Samuel took a nursing lamb and offered it as a whole burnt offering to the Lord. And Samuel cried out to the Lord for Israel, and the Lord answered him.

As Samuel was offering up the burnt offering, the Philistines drew near to attack Israel. But the Lord thundered with a mighty sound that day against the Philistines and threw them into confusion, and they were defeated before Israel.

And the men of Israel went out from Mizpah and pursued the Philistines and struck them, as far as below Beth-car.

Then Samuel took a stone and set it up between Mizpah and Shen and called its name Ebenezer; for he said, "Till now the Lord has helped us."

Day 1
Stone 1: Standing Stone
1 Samuel 7:5-12

I come before this Standing Stone
Full of sorrow and all alone,
As a broken child, I'm calling out to ya.
The stone reminds me of deeds you've done.
The battles fought, the vict'ries won
For all to see is written Alleluia.
Alleluia! Alleluia! Alleluia! Alleluia.

In many ancient cultures, standing stones held great significance. I remember the stelae that I saw in Tikal and Quirigua, Guatemala. Both were sites of significance in Mayan history. The stelae told the stories of different high priests and what had happened during their tenure as high priests. I was told that if the face of the priest and the staff were removed, it signified that that priest no longer held any power.

You may be familiar with the arch in the Roman Forum. It tells of Rome's many military victories, one of which was the destruction of Jerusalem. I'll never forget when I saw that arch. I was amazed when I saw engraved into the stone the image of a menorah being taken from a temple In this case, the stone spoke of the greatness of Rome over defiant Jerusalem.

In the case of the Bible reading, Samuel had set up a standing stone and had given it a name, Ebenezer (stone of help). This standing stone held a three part message. First, the name reminded future generations that the God of the Israelites is their help. Second, it reminded the Israelites of what God did that day. Third, it was a reminder to the Philistines of the defeat they suffered at the hand of the God of the Israelites.

Your grief journey will become a standing stone. It will take time with good days and bad days. It will be a testament to you that grief

4

will not have the final word. It will remind you of how God walked with you and strengthened you. Life was difficult and at times it seemed impossible, but God walked with you so that grief will not define who you are today. It will take time and it will be an up and down climb.

As a side note, before I decided to have each verse end with Halleluiah, this verse ended differently. "Of what I did for and through ya." Either way, your grief walk will become the standing stone. Your life will be a testament to what God has done in your life. Others will praise God as they see how he has worked in your life.

Prayer — O Lord, in order for a standing stone to be made, changes have to be made to the stone. The chisel needs to knock off pieces of the stone. It is painful and it is not easy. Be with me. Let me know that I am in your hands. Something beautiful waits at the end. You have not forgotten me. You truly are with me. In Jesus's name, amen.

Scripture Readings for Day 2:

Isaiah 25

On this mountain the LORD of hosts will make for all peoples
a feast of rich food, a feast of well-aged wine,
of rich food full of marrow, of aged wine well refined.
And he will swallow up on this mountain
the covering that is cast over all peoples,
the veil that is spread over all nations.
He will swallow up death forever;
and the Lord GOD will wipe away tears from all faces,
and the reproach of his people he will take away from all the
earth, for the LORD has spoken.
It will be said on that day,
"Behold, this is our God; we have waited for him, that he might
save us.
This is the LORD; we have waited for him;
let us be glad and rejoice in his salvation."

Isaiah 30

For a people shall dwell in Zion, in Jerusalem; you shall weep no
more. He will surely be gracious to you at the sound of your cry. As
soon as he hears it, he answers you. And though the Lord give you the
bread of adversity and the water of affliction, yet your Teacher will not
hide himself anymore, but your eyes shall see your Teacher. And your
ears shall hear a word behind you, saying, "This is the way, walk in it,"
when you turn to the right or when you turn to the left. Then you will
defile your carved idols overlaid with silver and your gold-plated metal
images. You will scatter them as unclean things. You will say to them,
"Be gone!"

Day 2
Standing Stone, Part 2
Isaiah 25:8 and Isaiah 30:19-22

Verse 2

I come to you with pain and fear
Struggling through this vale of tears
With just enough strength to cry out to ya.
But sadness is my one refrain.
A broken life is what remains.
Will there ever be another Alleluia?
(Hum)

Verse 3

You come to me in my brokenness
You recognize my pain and stress.
You whisper in my ear, "I am with ya."
You hold me in your warm embrace,
Gently wipe tears from my face
Assuring me you are my Alleluia.
Alleluia! Alleluia! Alleluia! Alleluia.

This is not a fun place to be. The sooner you can get out of it the better. I spent much too long in this place. Do not be confused. My faith did not waver during this time. I trusted in God, the problem was that the faith did not seem to be rewarded the way that I thought it would. I thought that I could use my faith and skip the whole grieving thing. I tried to jump over the pit, but I couldn't make it. I was blind to this reality. I lingered in the mire of unresolved grief. I was doing what was necessary to get through the day, but I did not deal with the consequences that my wife was gone. I had to come to grips with the ramifications of that truth in my life. For far too long, there was no joy and no sense that life would ever get better.

The healing began when I recognized that I was broken. I had become used to the loss and the sadness that comes with that loss. It seemed that this was how life was going to be. In saying the healing began, I do not say that I started *feeling*, but there was a sense of *freedom*. I no longer had to hold onto my world's problem all by myself. I hoped that the reason to praise God and the reason to celebrate this life would return. But it was not yet a reality in my life. That is the reason there is no Halleluiah that follows the question. I was not certain there would be a time of praise, a time I could say "God is good" with a conviction that the hearer (or even myself at times) would believe what I said.

The next verse tells of the first steps of the healing. I'm sure you are familiar with healing from a scraped knee or elbow. There comes a time when the scab itches. It does not feel good, but you know that your body is healing. The same is true with your spirit. The healing process is not easy. The best that can be said is that God is with you, not to protect you , not to prevent the healing process, but to sustain you. One of my favorite images in the Bible is of a compassionate God, who sees the suffering of his people and wipes the tears from their eyes. I can envision God with concern on his face, wanting to look me in the eye and tell me, "It's alright. I'm here. You'll be better." There will be another halleluiah, a reason to praise and serve me." In fact, God himself is my reason for praise.

Prayer — O Lord, sometimes it seems as the sadness will never end. There will never be another day to sing your praises with conviction. Comfort me with the certainty that you are with me every step of the way. It still hurts as I'm getting better. Open my eyes to see that you are with me. Amen

Scripture Readings for Day 3:

Mark 16

When the Sabbath was past, Mary Magdalene, Mary the mother of James, and Salome bought spices, so that they might go and anoint him.

And very early on the first day of the week, when the sun had risen, they went to the tomb. And they were saying to one another, "Who will roll away the stone for us from the entrance of the tomb?"

And looking up, they saw that the stone had been rolled back—it was very large. And entering the tomb, they saw a young man sitting on the right side, dressed in a white robe, and they were alarmed.

And he said to them, "Do not be alarmed. You seek Jesus of Nazareth, who was crucified. He has risen; he is not here. See the place where they laid him. But go, tell his disciples and Peter that he is going before you to Galilee. There you will see him, just as he told you."

And they went out and fled from the tomb, for trembling and astonishment had seized them, and they said nothing to anyone, for they were afraid.

Day 3

Stone 2 — The Stone at Jesus' Tomb

Mt 28, Mk 16, Luke 24, John 20

I come now to your burial tomb,
With no hope and full of gloom
I'm so saddened by what my sin did to ya.
The stone's been moved. The body's gone.
Death is dead. The vict'ry's won.
All is changed there's only alleluia.
Alleluia! Alleluia! Alleluia! Alleluia.

This verse refers to the early days of my grief walk. It is a reflection on the basis of my hope- the crucified and resurrected Lord. When death and the loss first strikes, it strikes hard. It strikes even harder when your life is entwined with the person who died. In reference to the women and the disciples, the loss went to another degree. Jesus was more than just a person. He was the Messiah. He was the person who the Jews had waited for over the centuries. He was the one who would put Jerusalem on the map again. His life ended up like all the other would be Messiahs from the past- a dead Messiah.

Their grief changed to joy in a second. The announcement of the angels changed the way they saw Jesus and how they saw death. A living Jesus made the people reflect on the things that He said earlier. Oh, that's what He meant when He said "Destroy this temple, and I will rebuilt it in three days." "I am the resurrection and the life." Death is not as scary as it used to be. Because Jesus is alive, I know that I will be alive with Him forever. Jesus is going to heaven to prepare a place for me.

At the present, the one thing this knowledge does give a person is perspective. It will not bring back my wife. I will not hear her voice again. I will never hold her in my arms again. I will not get another email. With all these nevers, there is perspective in the forever. The perspective comes from the empty tomb and the proclamation of the angels, "He is not here. He has risen as he said." The reality is that in this life my wife is gone and she will never come back. The perspective is but it's just for this life. My wife is with the Lord now. Death does not have the final say. My wife is living that truth. For now, my son and I are living the rest of our lives without his mother and my wife being able to impact our daily life, to talk to us, to be there with us, to celebrate and to cry with us.

But Jesus lives. It changes everything. My sadness has joy. My emptiness has fulfillment. My despair has hope. The crucified and resurrected Jesus is my Halleluiah, my reason to celebrate this broken life in which I find myself. Why? He lives and he gives life to all who come to the empty tomb and celebrate the empty tomb and the living Messiah.

Prayer — O Lord, I come to you with a broken life. Nothing I can do will ever fix it and make it whole. But I don't have to do anything. You did it all. You did it by dying for me. You did it by lying in the tomb. You did it by rising to life. You do it by coming to me and assuring me that you died and rose for me. Your life changes everything and your life changes me. Amen

Scripture Readings for Day 4:

Psalm 118

The stone that the builders rejected
    has become the cornerstone.
This is the LORD's doing;
    it is marvelous in our eyes.

Isaiah 28

Because you have said, "We have made a covenant with death,
    and with Sheol we have an agreement,
when the overwhelming whip passes through
    it will not come to us,
for we have made lies our refuge,
    and in falsehood we have taken shelter";
therefore thus says the Lord GOD,
"Behold, I am the one who has laid as a foundation in Zion,
    a stone, a tested stone,
a precious cornerstone, of a sure foundation:
    'Whoever believes will not be in haste.'

Matthew 21

Jesus said to them, "Have you never read in the Scriptures:
'The stone that the builders rejected has become the cornerstone;
this was the Lord's doing, and it is marvelous in our eyes'?"

Ephesians 2

So then you are no longer strangers and aliens, but you are fellow citizens with the saints and members of the household of God, built on the foundation of the apostles and prophets, Christ Jesus himself being the cornerstone, in whom the whole structure, being joined together, grows into a holy temple in the Lord. In him you also are being built together into a dwelling place for God by the Spirit.

Day 4

Stone 3: the Cornerstone

Psalm 118:22, Isaiah 28:16, Matthew 21:42, Ephesians 2:20

I come to you my cornerstone
Though you stand I struggle on.
At times it's so hard to just hang on to ya.
Yet you show up and you are near.
You speak to me, remove my fear
Calm comes back you restore my alleluia.
Alleluia! Alleluia! Alleluia! Alleluia.

The laying of the cornerstone is integral to the integrity of the building. This stone needs to get things off on the right start in order for the building to stand and not collapse. The cornerstone is the stone from which all the other stones are laid. Jesus is the cornerstone for many reasons. First, He is the Son of God. By His nature, He is holy and without sin. Second, He lived out His life in complete obedience to

the law. Third, He lived out that obedience not only by keeping the laws God had given, but by remaining obedient to the plan and purpose that His Father had given Him. Fourth, God rewarded that faithfulness by using it as the conduit of His grace. God's gifts come to us through Jesus, our crucified and risen Lord. Fifth, His work is not finished in us. He pleads our case in heaven and walks with us in our daily life.

Jesus is all that, but we are part of the building. I get in the way of what God is doing; and boy did I get in the way. Although I believe that Jesus is the Cornerstone, I did not always apply it to my life or give that voice a chance to comfort me. I focused on myself, my son, my life, but not on my Savior. That does not stop God from being who He is- our Rock. He is the immovable Rock when life is crumbling down. He is the high rock that we climb up when the water is rising. I love the image that Isaiah gives in Isaiah 30:19-21. The Lord, the Teacher, walks behind His people and speaks in their ears, "This is the way to go." I wish I would have done a better job of listening. When we listen, we hear the God of peace comfort us with His love and His presence.

This verse has us walking out of the pit. It is an uphill climg. There are times I feel like giving up. But God is with me. I hear the voice of God in the promises in the Bible, in my prayers, in the encouragement of others. This voice is so much more encouraging than the other voices which remind me of what I failure I am at times. God is my Halleluiah, my reminder that He is greater than all of this and that I am better than what I believe I am.

Prayer — O Lord, my cornerstone. Be my sure foundation on which my hope and my life are built. Be my protection, when I feel overwhelmed. Be my high place I can climb when troubles come surging. At all times help me to hear your voice as you whisper and guide me, so that I walk at peace with you through the troubles I face. In Jesus' name, amen.

14

Scripture Readings for Day 5:

Revelation 21

And I heard a loud voice from the throne saying, "Behold, the dwelling place of God is with man. He will dwell with them, and they will be his people, and God himself will be with them as their God. He will wipe away every tear from their eyes, and death shall be no more, neither shall there be mourning, nor crying, nor pain anymore, for the former things have passed away."

Revelation 3

Those whom I love, I reprove and discipline, so be zealous and repent. Behold, I stand at the door and knock. If anyone hears my voice and opens the door, I will come in to him and eat with him, and he with me.

Revelation 2

He who has an ear, let him hear what the Spirit says to the churches. To the one who conquers I will give some of the hidden manna, and I will give him a white stone, with a new name written on the stone that no one knows except the one who receives it.'

Day 5

Stone 4: Standing Stone, verse 6

Revelation 21:4; Revelation 3:20; 2:17

One day I'll stand before your throne.
When everything will be made known.
Those blazing eyes will be looking right through me.
The hand that wiped my tears away
Opened the door for me to stay,
Will give a stone with my new name "Alleluia".
Alleluia, Alleluia, Alleluia, Alleluia!

This verse celebrates the hope that transcends this life. Whether we are in the pit, on the mountain, on the plains, in the city, or at the beach, someday this day will come for each of us. The day we will be called home to be with our God. We will come before the throne of God. I pray that when I stand before the throne of God, I will hear the voice of my Lord say, "Well done, good and faithful servant."

Look at the triumvirate of promises. All these promises can be found in Revelation.

Revelation 21:4 — In addition to the great promise of wiping the tears away, there is an even greater promise. There will be no more reason to cry. Death will be no more. Separation from our loved ones will be over. The reason is clear and certain. Sin and death will have had their season. They were conquered by the cross and the empty tomb. The hands that will wipe away our tears will have scars.

Revelation 3:20 — You may be familiar with the painting of Jesus standing at the door and knocking. In this image, there is no door knob to open the door. It has to be opened by the person inside. The beauty of the image is that Jesus is the One who comes to the closed door and invites us to spend time with him. My life is so different because He came to me. My life is so much richer because He makes Himself at home with me and stays with me. When we are together, we eat together, as families do. I have fond memories of the family dinner table and the conversations we would have. This is the intimate relationship that Jesus has with his people. So when I stand before the throne of God, gazing into the blazing eyes, those eyes recognize me because we have shared time and meal time together.

Revelation 2:17— The white stone with a new name is a beautiful reflection of the religious life of the Jew. Once a year, a chosen priest would enter the Holy of Holies. The opportunity would be given to the priests in a certain village or area. It was a once in a lifetime opportunity. How did the priests pick out who would serve? The name of each priest was written on a white stone, and the priest whose name was written on that stone would serve. Not only will all be chosen to serve, but all will be given a new name. Simon was renamed Peter (Rock). Levi was renamed Matthew (Gift of God). In the song, my new name will be Halleluiah. I will serve God, not one day but every day. I will be renamed by my Lord, who sees me as I truly am, not as I see myself.

Prayer — O Lord, thank you for what your hands have done for me. They wipe away my tears, knock on and open the door, break bread, lift a cup, write my name and hand me a stone. As much as I look forward to seeing your handiwork, I look forward to seeing you face to face. In Jesus' name.

Scripture Readings for Day 6:

Job 1

Then Job arose and tore his robe and shaved his head and fell on the ground and worshiped. And he said, "Naked I came from my mother's womb, and naked shall I return. The Lord gave, and the Lord has taken away; blessed be the name of the Lord."

The Day that My Heart Stood Still

The day began like any other
On a Sunday, I will never forget.
The particulars I do not recall.
Church in the morning, afternoon drinks.
Snoring sent me out of the bedroom
Then everything started to go wrong.
She complained about her head aches
That her vision was not right.
When I held her in my arms, she collapsed.
It was the day that my heart stood still.

The days that followed were a fog.
One day to the next, just getting by.
Living for my son, not caring for myself.
Trying to make sure he was happy.
The mail started piling up.
I stopped watering plants, no gardens.
Meals were a chore, more for my son than me.
The Christmas letters were never sent.
Going through life without joy or desire.
Changed by the day that my heart stood still.

Things went from bad to worse
After we moved from the house we shared.
Memories packed, stored away and discarded.
Living in a place that was not our own.
The stress piled up and the sleep got worse
Pressures mounted up from all sides.
The day came that started the freefall.
I was told that I would no longer be working here.
Now with no wife, no job, no direction.
The rubble from the day that my heart stood still.

Yes, she's gone but she's not forgotten.
Sure, there's a loss from a love too soon taken.
But I refuse to let that loss tarnish her memory.
I will not let her loss make me lose.
Her love made me whole and still does.
My son is a reminder of what we began.
Death has made us part but life goes on.
It goes on with the promise of before.
Made strong by the love that we shared
Not ruled by the day that my heart stood still.

Day 6
The Day My Heart Stood Still
Job 1:20, 21

Death is a reality that everyone will face sometime. Death is a reality that will strike close to home. This is a truth that we know and accept but for which we are never prepared. This is especially true if the person that we love dies suddenly. When a loved one dies, we are never ready for the moment. No matter how many days, weeks, months, or years that person struggles with his or her disease we are never ready when it happens. Although we may have time to prepare, we also struggle as we see the vibrant person waste away over time. The benefit of a sudden death is that one will always remember the loved person as full of life and full of energy. Either way, we are left unprepared for the emotions that will overwhelm us.

A strange thing for me is that I remember the moment she died as if it were yesterday. The next days, weeks, and months afterwards are a fog. Why? That is the moment that everything changed. That was the day that I went from coherent to incoherent, from functioning to non-functional.

Job, when he was confronted with the death of his children, was very stoic. "The Lord gives and the Lord takes away, blessed be the name of the Lord." It is very important to hold on to your faith when you are completely devastated. It is also very important to deal with your grief. Someday your grief will catch up to you if you do not deal with it. In my case, I let taking care of my son and taking care of the church blind me from taking care of myself. Eventually this caught up to me and I'm still living with the consequences. No matter when you deal with the grief be assured that you will not be facing that grief alone. God will be with you. Your family and friends want to walk with you through this as well.

Also be sure of this; that day will be a defining moment in your life. Just don't let it redefine you in your future. This day will change

20

your life, and it will change you. But it does not have to change your foundation. There is a constant that does not change. It was the constant that was true before your life changed. God is the same yesterday, today, and forever. The steadfast love of the Lord lasts forever. The God who loved you before loves you now. But more importantly, the God who was with you before is with you now and he will see you through this.

Prayer — O Lord, questions and confusion are racing in my mind. I have no idea what is going on. Please surround me with friends who will be with me and will pray for me. Please give me the strength and the endurance to confront the pain and the loss. My life has changed and will never be the same. But You are the same and You never change. Even in my loss, You love me. You are with me. You comfort me. Give me strength as I deal with my changed life. In Jesus' name, amen.

Scripture Readings for Day 7:

Genesis 35

Then they journeyed from Bethel. When they were still some distance from Ephrath, Rachel went into labor, and she had hard labor. And when her labor was at its hardest, the midwife said to her, "Do not fear, for you have another son." And as her soul was departing (for she was dying), she called his name Ben-oni; but his father called him Benjamin. So Rachel died, and she was buried on the way to Ephrath (that is, Bethlehem), and Jacob set up a pillar over her tomb. It is the pillar of Rachel's tomb, which is there to this day. Israel journeyed on and pitched his tent beyond the tower of Eder.

What do I tell my son?

What do I tell my son?
When in an instant his mom is gone?
When she can no longer play with him?
She'll never hug him again?

Chorus
She loved you to the end.
She loves you in heaven now.
She's in heaven now waiting.
She's praying we get through somehow.

"The doctors couldn't help her.
Her brain broke no repair.
It was not what she wanted.
Never think she didn't care."

What do I tell my son?
As side by side, we struggle on.
When so different is our life
Without his mom, my wife.
Each holiday seems shallow
In the joy, there's a shadow.
In the laughter, there's a void.
A wallow, I can't avoid.

What do I tell my son?
As we continue to carry on?
"Thank God that we're together."
"We're a team through stormy weather."
"God's with us and we'll make it."
"Whatever comes, we'll take it."

O Lord, you have us in your hands
And you'll never let us go.
You wipe away our every tear
And you want us to know.
You're right by our side.
In your love, we abide.
That's what I tell my son.

Day 7
What do I tell my son?
Genesis 35:16-20

One of the most difficult parts of living without my wife is that my son is also living without his mom. That leaves me to do the impossible. I try to be both his dad and mom. The sooner I realize that this is not possible, the sooner a weight will be taken off my shoulders. I'm not sure that I have learned it yet. I am just being asked to be his father without a mother. I will never be able to fill his mother's place. But I can and need to make sure that the roles that his mother played in his life are accomplished.

But that does not erase the questions and the void that is left in my son's life. His mother's death was his first encounter with death. None of our cats had died. No close or distant family member had died. There were some deaths in the church, but nobody who had an impact on his daily life. His first encounter with death was the closest person to him who had the greatest impact on him.

I think the greatest mistake that I made for my son and for myself in the weeks and months after Jill's death was that I wanted to keep my son happy. This sounded like an admirable goal, but it avoided a reality. We were both hurting. We both had lost someone very near to us. She was the person who was closest to each of us. I knew that I was hurting. He was hurting too. I gave him a false message, which was life continues the same when your world has collapsed around you.

What I did tell my son was the foundation of our faith. "Mommy is with Jesus." I can tell him that because of what Jesus taught and because of what He did. Jesus said "I am the resurrection and the life." He demonstrated that by coming back to life. Jesus said "I am the bread of life. He who eats of this bread and drinks of this cup will never die. And I will raise him up on the last day." He was raised up from the dead. Jill trusted that promise made by our faithful God.

Prayer — Lord, I am not the only one who grieved when my loved one died. I thank you for giving me such a precious person to grieve. Help me first to cry with those you have placed in my life. Help me to honor the importance of the person who is no longer a part of our lives. Help me to also hold on to those precious promises. Help me to instill that confident hope that I have in my child, so that we do not grieve like those who have no hope. In Jesus' name, amen.

Scripture Readings for Day 8:

John 11

Now when Jesus came, he found that Lazarus had already been in the tomb four days. Bethany was near Jerusalem, about two miles off, and many of the Jews had come to Martha and Mary to console them concerning their brother. So when Martha heard that Jesus was coming, she went and met him, but Mary remained seated in the house. Martha said to Jesus, "Lord, if you had been here, my brother would not have died. But even now I know that whatever you ask from God, God will give you." Jesus said to her, "Your brother will rise again." Martha said to him, "I know that he will rise again in the resurrection on the last day." Jesus said to her, "I am the resurrection and the life. Whoever believes in me, though he die, yet shall he live, and everyone who lives and believes in me shall never die. Do you believe this?" She said to him, "Yes, Lord; I believe that you are the Christ, the Son of God, who is coming into the world."

When she had said this, she went and called her sister Mary, saying in private, "The Teacher is here and is calling for you." And when she heard it, she rose quickly and went to him. Now Jesus had not yet come into the village, but was still in the place where Martha had met him. When the Jews who were with her in the house, consoling her, saw Mary rise quickly and go out, they followed her, supposing that she was going to the tomb to weep there. Now when Mary came to where Jesus was and saw him, she fell at his feet, saying to him, "Lord, if you had been here, my brother would not have died." When Jesus saw her weeping, and the Jews who had come with her also weeping, he was deeply moved in his spirit and greatly troubled. And he said, "Where have you laid him?" They said to him, "Lord, come and see." Jesus wept. So the Jews said, "See how he loved him!" But some of them said, "Could not he who opened the eyes of the blind man also have kept this man from dying?"

I'm Holding to the Promise

I believe in the Holy Spirit, Holy Christian Church,
The Communion of Saints, The forgiveness of Sins
The Resurrection of the Body, and life everlasting

What happens when your foundation's shaken?
When your confidence seems so unsure?
The life that seemed like the American dream
Is now broken there is no cure.
The days had rhyme and reason
But that reason has been taken away.
She, who was the heartbeat of the home,
Has stopped breathing. O Lord I pray.

Chorus
Lord, I'm holding to the promise.
You are the resurrection the life.
Though we die, we will live with you.
That's the promise for all and for my wife.
Though I know the promise is certain.
At times, it's so hard to believe.
Day by day, hoping against all hope.
Trusting when it's time to grieve.

Where do I look to when I feel no joy?
When I talk of faith but there is no reward?
Day by day, it's the same routine.
Trusting His word, but dull is the sword.
In spite of all, I still look to that Word.
For the Word is certain and so is our God.
When I look to myself and hope to find peace,
I do not find joy only a rod, only a rod.

So I hold on to the things I know are true
I believe in the Spirit, I believe in His Word
I believe in the Church, I believe what I heard
I believe in forgiveness, in a life that is new.
I believe, I believe in God. Yes, I do!

Day 8
I'm Holding to the Promise
John 11:17-37

A good friend of mine mentioned how the liturgy had helped him after a close high school friend had died. I did the same thing. As I dealt with the initial drama and shock of Jill's death, the words of the Apostles' Creed kept running through my head. "I believe in the Holy Spirit, the Holy Christian Church, the Communion of Saints, the forgiveness of sins, the resurrection and the life, and life everlasting." My life was shaken, and I needed something solid on which to stand. So I held to the promise of the resurrected life.

A verse that was a mantra running through my mind was the promise that Jesus spoke to sisters, Mary and Martha, when their brother, Lazarus, died. "I am the Resurrection and the Life; he who believes in me, though he die, yet shall he live." Jill loved the Lord. She was a faithful servant of God and a wonderful partner in ministry. She did not like to be in the spotlight, but everything she did was done joyfully to serve the Lord. I have no doubt that she is in heaven celebrating with the saints. I am certain of this, not because she was a faithful person, but because she served a faithful God. This faithful God made a promise. In life and in death, we held to the promises of God. In good and in bad, we know that God is faithful.

I did not and I could not put my confidence in anything else than the goodness of God, his faithfulness, and his promises. He was willing to put those promises on paper so that He could be held accountable. He is faithful and cannot deny himself. The empty tomb and the living Lord change everything, even the way we consider the darkest times in our lives, the hour of death of our loved ones. As dark and devastating as those times are, there is hope because Jesus lives.

We have hope, but we still grieve. Jill was a lovely person. My life and my love revolved around this woman that the Lord gave to me to be my wife. There will always be a hole in my life. There will always be a "Jill piece" missing from my life. At the same time Jesus says, "I am the resurrection and the life, he who believes in me though he die, yet shall he live." I'm holding the faithful God to be true to that message.

Prayer — O Lord, you are the resurrection and the life. Thank you for what you give me to hold on to when I am devastated by the loss of a loved one. I believe in the Holy Spirit, the Holy Christian Church, the Communion of Saints, the Forgiveness of sins, the resurrection and the life, and life everlasting. Amen.

Scripture Readings for Day 9:

Psalm 34

The eyes of the LORD are toward the righteous
    and his ears toward their cry.
The face of the LORD is against those who do evil,
    to cut off the memory of them from the earth.
When the righteous cry for help, the LORD hears
    and delivers them out of all their troubles.
The LORD is near to the brokenhearted
    and saves the crushed in spirit.
Many are the afflictions of the righteous,
    but the LORD delivers him out of them all.
He keeps all his bones;
    not one of them is broken.
Affliction will slay the wicked,
    and those who hate the righteous will be condemned.
The LORD redeems the life of his servants;
    none of those who take refuge in him will be condemned.

Two Halves Make a Hole

"You are my W", I told my future wife.
"I had a hole, but now I'm whole."
The start of a brand new life.

They say 2 halves make a whole
But that's not my reality.
Two halves make a hole.
There's a hole inside of me.

Too soon she was gone, Taken away from me.
Lost and all alone. Life is just a loan.
That's my new reality

The hole left behind, can't have the final say.
I'll become whole now from this hole.
Love guides me day to day.

Two halves become a hole
And there are lessons to be learned
Two halves become a whole.
A stronger heart is earned.

Day 9
Two Halves make a whole
Psalm 34:15-22

A broken heart is terrible kick in the gut. It is amazing how much it hurts, even though nothing is physically damaged. It sure feels though like your whole insides have been run through the wringer.

God said something amazing to Adam when he first saw Eve.. "The two will become one." That is the wonder of a marriage blessed by God. You go from living a life of "me" to a life of "us". Your interests cease being self-serving to a life of serving others. This happens even more when a child comes into the picture. This is the beauty of becoming a husband and a father. Your life is no longer your own, but it is much richer.

That is why when that part of your life is taken away, it hurts so much. During the nearly thirteen years that we shared together, our lives became so entwined. Jill was better than I deserved. I devoted my life to her. The Lord took her from me so suddenly that I had no time to prepare myself to the adjustment that was thrust upon me. Even if I had time, the result would have been the same. I would still be without Jill. I would still be lacking my "W" who made me whole.

There is a lesson that takes a long time to learn. I don't think I have learned it yet. There is only One who makes you whole. It is not the people who are in your life, not even your spouse. It is the One who has put those people in your life. God, who has put these people in your life, has put them in your life for a time. God is in our lives for eternity.

Even more importantly, God is the one who truly makes you whole. He truly is your "W". I thank Him so much that Jill was in my life for all those years as my wife. I wish I had many more years with her. But my Lord has been a part of my life for as long as I can remember. My Lord has been my reason for waking up in the morning and me blessing when I go to bed a night. I have dedicated my life to serving Him and His people. But more importantly, He has dedicated His life to serving His people. He is the one who came and lived among us. He is the one who emptied Himself and took the form of a servant. He is the one who showed the greatest love and gave His life for me. He is the one who took my sin on his shoulders and received the condemnation that I deserve. He is the one who took my judgment. He is the one who rose and stood before me and said "Peace be with you. Your sins are forgiven." I am the One who took your life, which was a hole, and I made it whole.

Prayer — Lord, thank you for bringing the people that you have brought into my life. Especially I thank you for bringing (Jill) into my life. My life was made so much richer through (her). But Lord, my life is truly made whole by You. You are the one who brings me peace. You are the one who brings me joy. You are the one who makes me whole. Forgive me when I replace You with the ones you have brought into my life. Thank you for bringing these people into my life and the impact that they have had and the love that they have shared. They were gifts that You gave me for a time, so that I may love and understand You better. In Jesus' name. Amen

Scripture Readings for Day 10:

Psalm 102

Hear my prayer, O LORD;
    let my cry come to you!
Do not hide your face from me
    in the day of my distress!
Incline your ear to me;
    answer me speedily in the day when I call!
For my days pass away like smoke,
    and my bones burn like a furnace.
My heart is struck down like grass and has withered;
    I forget to eat my bread.

Because of my loud groaning
    my bones cling to my flesh.
I am like a desert owl of the wilderness,
    like an owl of the waste places;
I lie awake;
    I am like a lonely sparrow on the housetop.
All the day my enemies taunt me;
    those who deride me use my name for a curse.
For I eat ashes like bread
    and mingle tears with my drink,
because of your indignation and anger;
    for you have taken me up and thrown me down.
My days are like an evening shadow;
    I wither away like grass.

Isaiah 40:6-8

In sacrifice and offering you have not delighted,
    but you have given me an open ear.
Burnt offering and sin offering
    you have not required.
Then I said, "Behold, I have come;
    in the scroll of the book it is written of me:
I delight to do your will, O my God;
    your law is within my heart."

What Will Never Be

There's a void in each celebration,
A space no one else can ever fill.
Reminders of how much my life changes.
But images of you are standing still.
Our memories are now cast in stone
As we go through life now all alone.
Our boy is growing up day by day.
But you won't be with us along the way.

Chorus
Anniversaries are but a reminder
Of what now will never be.
Life goes on and we are growing.
But these steps you'll never see.
We won't grow old together side by side.
No happy every after for you my bride.
You'll never see his graduation day.
You won't be with us along the way.

His lost teeth are starting to grow in.
His baseball skills are getting better.
Moved on from Angry Birds to Pokémon.
He now loves to watch the weather.
He still crawls into our bed at night.
And loves to cuddle when he can.
We're still going to the splash pads.
Our small boy is growing into a man.

You're not there to take the pictures
At each year's first day of classes.
And you won't see his graduation day
The changes as each year passes.
You won't be there when he makes his vows.
He'll never be led by your wise advice.
He won't again hear the joy of your laugh.
But he remembers the love in your voice.

Day 10
What Will Never Be
Psalm 102:1-11 Isaiah 40:6-8

One of the realities of the death of your loved one is that your memories with that person have come to an end. Though they are beautiful memories, you will not make any new ones. Now it is true that you will neither have any sad or regrettable memories either. There will no longer be any new memories with that person in them.

This reality is more poignant when a child is young. There are so many milestones that Jill will miss. For Marco this is sad too because Mommy will not be by his side. Most of his other friends have both sets of parents there celebrating them. Marco is going through life without one of the most significant people in a person's life.

I cannot say that I'll never forget Marco's first birthday without his mom because the truth is I was still going through the fog. I remember we had a bounce house and a waterslide. We also had Angry Bird stuff everywhere. I also remember that I only took one or two pictures because my camera was not charged. This is a detail that would have been attended to by Jill. Every birthday since has been far short of what it would be if Jill was organizing it. They are fun because I make sure that somehow there is water involved. But when the big days arrive, either anniversaries or life milestones, it rings hollow because Jill is not there.

It is easy to focus on what I don't have that most of the rest of the world has. But when I focus on what I don't have, I am putting myself in a precarious position from the beginning. I am beginning with a negative, and more than likely that is where I am going to end up. In my thinking, I will either end up as a victim, an object of pity, or a hero who is doing incredible in spite of the circumstances. It doesn't matter how often I hear people say what a good job I am doing; I do not feel like I am doing a good job. I know how much better his life would be with his mother. This is where I end up when this is my mindset.

It is important for your mental wellbeing to consider what you do have. Consider who you are. You are a child of God fearfully and wonderfully made. God has blessed you with this child and he or she calls you his parent. A special bond has been formed in a large part because of this tragedy in your life. He is now dependent on you and you alone. But more importantly, remember when you are weak and feel like you have failed, you have God. Better stated, God has you. God has not forgotten or forsaken you. God has not placed too much on your plate. God is with you and will get you through this. You have family and friends. You are not alone unless you have closed yourself off from the people in your life. Many of these friends and family members want to help and are just waiting for the chance to do so. You have the privilege of carrying all your cares to God in prayer. You have the assurance that sins are forgiven and relationships are restored. You have love- love for your child, your child's love for you, God's love- and the promise that love covers a multitude of sins.

Prayer — O Lord, help me not to focus on what I don't have and what will never be. Help me to trust you with what is and what you have given me. Help us to live in the truth that your grace is sufficient for me.

Scripture Readings for Day 11:

Psalm 6

I am weary with my moaning;
    every night I flood my bed with tears;
    I drench my couch with my weeping.
My eye wastes away because of grief;
    it grows weak because of all my foes.
Depart from me, all you workers of evil,
    for the LORD has heard the sound of my weeping.
The LORD has heard my plea;
    the LORD accepts my prayer.

The Voices in the Night

The voices in the night refuse to give me rest
They keep my mind occupied. Man they are a test.
Relentlessly, they make me churn through ev'ry word
Reenacting each moment and things I thought I heard.

These demons in my closet, their purpose is exact.
To reinvent reality — make their lies the fact.
These voices I do not trust, but oh they have my ear.
The more I toss and turn in bed, the more I'm filled with fear.

You are a failure.   You have no worth.
They all hate you.   Fall off the earth
You have no money.   You blew it bad.
You're good for nothing.   You made them sad.
You've been betrayed.   None you can trust.
You are the victim.   All you do is lust.
You'll never succeed.   You are a bum.
    Just go back to the place where you are from.

These voices do not tire, every night the same.
Every night a different look, but it's the same old game.
But the truth is that I do have a choice.
Lord, please speak up. I need to hear your voice.

Day 11
The Voices in the Night
Psalm 6:6-9

After we moved, my routine was upset. This had ramifications for which I was not prepared, one of which was my sleep pattern. Now, sleeping on a futon for five months did not help, but there was more happening. Thankfully, I could go to sleep with no problem. The problem was what happened after I woke up during the night. I could not get back to sleep. Thoughts and ideas raced through my mind. Some of these thoughts were work related and what had to be done soon. The majority were thoughts of how bad my life was getting and how much I had messed things up. At the worst time, I was only sleeping three to four hours a night. I would start to pray, but then my restless thoughts would take over. The rest of the time was spent either tossing or turning in bed with those thoughts or watching TV, hoping that would help me sleep.

My counselor taught me a breathing technique to help calm those restless thoughts. As I slowly breathed in I would say in my head, "God's". As I exhaled, I would think, "Peace." This did help me. I could sleep after ten to fifteen minutes.

But then the sleepless nights returned. I remember one night when things were getting particularly bad. I told the "voices", (my restless thoughts), "If you are going to keep me awake, I am going to use this time to write titles for poems." The idea of this book was born. After I wrote down a few titles, I was able to go to sleep again. After a few nights and about twelve titles, my sleep returned. When the sleepless nights returned, I continued this process.

One of the promises of God that I would pray during the restless times was this verse from 1 Peter, "5:[6] Humble yourselves, therefore, under the mighty hand of God so that at the proper time he may exalt you, [7] casting all your anxieties on him, because he cares for you." Part of the trouble that I face when I have the racing thoughts is that I think that I can resolve it if I examine it logically. First, at that time, I am not thinking logically or coherently. Second, I am cutting myself off from my greatest resource. I shorten the hand of God and think my hand can do a better job. That is why the teaching begins by saying, "Be Humble!" The way I humble myself is by casting my cares on God. I say to God, "I can't do this by myself. I need you." The peace that came after this was amazing. That was the voice I needed to hear.

Prayer- O Lord, when the voices in the night come, help me to understand why they come. Help me understand that they are meant to separate me from you and to separate me from myself. I question Your goodness and Your plan for me. I question myself, my value, and my abilities. More importantly, help me to humble myself and turn to You wholeheartedly, knowing that only You can help. Help me to appreciate the help You send. Help me to appreciate all that You have made me to be. More than anything help me to hear Your voice and go where You lead. In Jesus' name, amen.

Scripture Readings for Day 12:

Psalm 39

"And now, O Lord, for what do I wait?
    My hope is in you.
Deliver me from all my transgressions.
    Do not make me the scorn of the fool!
I am mute; I do not open my mouth,
    for it is you who have done it.
Remove your stroke from me;
    I am spent by the hostility of your hand.
When you discipline a man
    with rebukes for sin,
you consume like a moth what is dear to him;
    surely all mankind is a mere breath! Selah
Hear my prayer, O LORD,
    and give ear to my cry;
    hold not your peace at my tears!
For I am a sojourner with you,
    a guest, like all my fathers.
Look away from me, that I may smile again,
    before I depart and am no more!"

Fragile Peace

I hope you don't know what I'm saying.
I hope that you don't understand.
That place between hope deprived
And sadness that has no end.
That emptiness that sucks all joy.
That place that deprives all cheer.
Where sleep does not have a chance.
And dreams? They never appear.

Chorus
The joy's short lived.
The hope is brief.
The calm never gives me release.
My smile won't last
My laughter's short.
All I sense is fragile peace.

The day goes well. Then I go to bed.
I hit the pillow and it hits back.
The fact is clear. I'm on my own.
The one I love, her place is black
We shared the day at end of day.
The silence louder than any shout.
I lay there as quiet pounds my head.
Reminds me of who I live without

Day 12
Fragile Peace
Psalm 39:7-13

The reality of grief is that it is a wild roller coaster ride. At first, you have your bad days and your worse days. Even those days which seem to go well at first can come crashing down by the simplest thing: a favorite song; driving by your favorite restaurant; or you hear somebody calling out your wife's name.

This time is very difficult. It is made more difficult if you isolate yourself away from family and friends. It is more difficult if you hold your grief in or avoid it, either by focusing on others rather than yourself or losing yourself in work.

As you go through this time, there is something that you crave,: stability. Your life had footing while you lived life with your loved one. Now that the person is gone, you question everything. Your life seemed complete. Now all you see is a big gaping hole in your house, in your life, in your heart.

The Hebrew language is a picture language. The Hebrew word, shalom or peace, paints the picture of something being whole or complete. If something is missing or not complete, there is no peace. It is kind of like a jigsaw puzzle that has a missing piece. All you see is that empty space where a piece should be.

Your life has a missing piece. As long as you focus or dwell on that missing piece, there will be no peace. Whenever the loss of that piece is brought to your attention, whatever peace you had will be broken.

So what's the answer? How do we ever get that peace back? The first step is to recognize and realize that we are not the ones who produce the peace. I was not at peace because Jill was my wife, although, yes, she did make my life complete. I was at peace because God was the center of our home. He is the one that brought Jill and Marco into my life. He is the reason that I woke up in the morning and went to bed

44

at night. This peace was His gift to me and all those who lived in the house. Though my life has changed, God has not changed. All these things have not changed- my God, His love, His word, His grace, His plan for me.

I still struggle. But when I am with God, I have peace. When I pray, I have peace. When my focus is on God and not on myself, I have peace.

Prayer — Lord, the time of peace is short and fleeting. I need to wrestle with the significance of my loved one's death. I also need to crawl up in Your lap and cry. While there, I need to give it all to You, knowing that You will restore my peace and my hope. In Jesus' name. Amen

Scripture Readings for Day 13:

Psalm 77

I cry aloud to God,
    aloud to God, and he will hear me.
In the day of my trouble I seek the Lord;
    in the night my hand is stretched out without wearying;
    my soul refuses to be comforted.
When I remember God, I moan;
    when I meditate, my spirit faints. Selah
You hold my eyelids open;
    I am so troubled that I cannot speak.
I consider the days of old,
    the years long ago.
I said, "Let me remember my song in the night;
    let me meditate in my heart."
    Then my spirit made a diligent search:
"Will the Lord spurn forever,

and never again be favorable?
Has his steadfast love forever ceased?
    Are his promises at an end for all time?
Has God forgotten to be gracious?
    Has he in anger shut up his compassion?" Selah
Then I said, "I will appeal to this,
    to the years of the right hand of the Most High."
I will remember the deeds of the LORD;
    yes, I will remember your wonders of old.
I will ponder all your work,
    and meditate on your mighty deeds.
Your way, O God, is holy.
    What god is great like our God?
You are the God who works wonders;
    you have made known your might among the peoples.
You with your arm redeemed your people,
    the children of Jacob and Joseph. Selah
When the waters saw you, O God,
    when the waters saw you, they were afraid;
    indeed, the deep trembled.
The clouds poured out water;
    the skies gave forth thunder;
    your arrows flashed on every side.
The crash of your thunder was in the whirlwind;
    your lightnings lighted up the world;
    the earth trembled and shook.
Your way was through the sea,
    your path through the great waters;
    yet your footprints were unseen.
You led your people like a flock
    by the hand of Moses and Aaron.

Unwelcomed Guest

You came here unannounced,
Unwelcomed I might add.
You walked into my life.
Since then things went bad.
You came without permission.
Your agenda was quite clear.
I had no strength to cast you out.
But I want you out of here.

Chorus
You are an unwelcomed guest.
You are a constant pest.
You are not welcome here.
You are the sum of fear.
Oh, how I want you gone.
Please, just leave me alone.

You came here with your baggage
That you wanted me to bear.
You unloaded every weapon
Without a single care.
Took advantage of my weakness.
Caught me when I was down.
Made sure that joy and peace
Were nowhere to be found.

Made sure I was lonely
And pity filled my head
Despair in the kitchen
Sorrow was in my bed.
Anger filled the household
Fear was in the air.
Lord, I just can't take it.
On you, I cast my care

Lord, get this strongman out.
And clean the garbage now.
This guest has stayed too long.
I need him gone and how.
Replace him with your Spirit.
I need to know your gifts.
Your love, your joy, your gentleness.
And hope that my soul lifts.

Day 13
Unwelcomed Guest
Psalm 77

When grief takes over and depression is not far away, you look at yourself, and you wonder who that is in the mirror. You wonder "how did I ever come to this place in my life?" You wonder why faith is not working.

At this stage, there is no happiness in the present, and there is no happy ever after. Any consolation and hope that is given finds no footing because there is not inner strength. Your self-worth and self-confidence are not assets because when you look at yourself, all you see if how you have messed things up and how you have failed.

The important thing to remember is that this is just a stage. Yes, it is a painful stage, and it is a stage that seems to have no end and no hope. Even though it may look hopeless, I placed my hope in the One who defeated death. The One who said that He would not leave me desolate is fighting by my side. He also told me that in this world there would be tribulation, but He has overcome the world.

The only good news in this is that you do not place your hope on how you feel. You also should not place your despair on how you feel. There is someone who transcends all of this. Nothing can separate us from the love of God. In Christ, we are more than conquerors. Even when we feel like we have been taken hostage and tied up and completely vulnerable, Jesus is the same yesterday, today, and forever. Your feelings can deceive you but the promises of God are faithful.

The only good news is the only news that you need. Keep your eyes on Jesus during this time. He is the light in the darkness. He is the shepherd who walks beside you. He is the friend of sinners who comes to you where you are. You are invited by our Lord to cast your cares on Him because He cares for you. He is faithful. He is the one who began a good work in you, and He will bring it to completion.

Prayer — Lord, sometimes the only thing that I have to hold on to is You. Hope has no consolation. My life seems to have no value and I have lost my purpose. Lord, be with me. Help me as the strong man seems to be having his way in my life. But You are the one who sets me free. Be with me now, and restore to me the joy of Your salvation. In Jesus' name, amen.

Scripture Readings for Day 14:

Psalm 30

I will extol you, O LORD, for you have drawn me up
    and have not let my foes rejoice over me.
O LORD my God, I cried to you for help,
    and you have healed me.
O LORD, you have brought up my soul from Sheol;
    you restored me to life from among those who go down to the
    pit.
Sing praises to the LORD, O you his saints,
    and give thanks to his holy name.
For his anger is but for a moment,
    and his favor is for a lifetime.
Weeping may tarry for the night,
    but joy comes with the morning.
As for me, I said in my prosperity,
    "I shall never be moved."
By your favor, O LORD,
    you made my mountain stand strong;
you hid your face;
    I was dismayed.

To you, O LORD, I cry,
    and to the Lord I plead for mercy:
"What profit is there in my death,
    if I go down to the pit?
Will the dust praise you?
    Will it tell of your faithfulness?
Hear, O LORD, and be merciful to me!
    O LORD, be my helper!"
You have turned for me my mourning into dancing;
    you have loosed my sackcloth
    and clothed me with gladness,
that my glory may sing your praise and not be silent.
    O LORD my God, I will give thanks to you forever!

Walking into the Canyon

Step by step, I walked down into the canyon,
Not realizing how far I had gone.
I was distracted by what was around me.
Not thinking about what I'd done.
I'd walked so far and came so far down.
Can't believe I covered so much ground.

Chorus
Now I'm walking at the base of the canyon.
Not knowing if I'm ever coming out.
My muscles ache. Oh how my legs shake.
I look up, and there's nothing but doubt.
Cuz I'm walking at the base of the canyon.
And the heat is taking its toll.
My body's spent, and all my hope just went
Out of my spirit and out of my soul.

As I walked down the canyon, I gave no thought
Where the decisions I made might take me.
But the truth is that I could not think at all.
Not knowing that this path it would break me.
I look back and I wonder what I was thinking
Without thought down I was sinking,

I don't want to stay at the base of the canyon.
I need the resolve to find my way out.
Step by step I walk, my fears I face.
Confronting my confusion, pain, and doubt.
Knowing that although the road will be tough,
With You by my side that is enough.

Step by step I walk, and You give me strength.
I stop to catch my breath. You breathe in me.
My body and throat are dry, can't be quenched.
I stop for a drink. You give the water that flows free.
The sun beats down on me, saps my strength.
You provide shadow, a shelter to comfort me.
The ascent doesn't seem so far the longer we walk.
The doubts in my head aren't so strong, the longer we talk.
Thank you for walking with me out of the canyon.

Day 14
Walking into the Canyon
Psalm 30, Psalm 143

I have walked across the Grand Canyon three times. There are lessons from that hike that apply to one's grief walk. They definitely applied to mine.

One of the basic principles when one hikes a canyon is to know that it takes twice as long to hike out than it does to hike into the canyon. Sadly, it took a while to recognize that I was in a downward spiral. Before I realized it, I was far down in the canyon, and I had a lot of climbing to do to get out. The ascent out was just beginning.

The descent down the canyon is relatively easy. Sure your upper leg muscles are chewed up, but once you walk on the level ground at the base of the canyon that is quickly relieved. Even so, when you start climbing out of the canyon, you have already expended a lot of energy and you go up already having expended a good bit of energy. The same is true for your climb out of grief. By the time that you get to the bottom of your grief, you are spent emotionally. Sadness has paid its toll on your emotional wellbeing. Doubt and despair have sapped you spiritually. Sleepless nights and stress have weakened you physically. You do not have the energy to climb out that you had at the beginning.

Never forget the psychological struggle that goes on inside the head. It can seem overwhelming to think about how far you have to go when you first look up and see how high the canyon ridge is. When you assess your personal resources, you may wonder if you will ever get out of your situation, and if you will be able to climb out of the canyon.

Then you remember that step by step you came to where you are now, and step by step you will get out this situation. There are some things that you brought in your backpack that will help you as you climb out of the valley. Your most important asset is water. You need to keep yourself hydrated, or, at best, someone will be carrying you out of the canyon. Spiritually, this happens as you remember that you have the Living Water (John 7:37-39). As Jesus explains, the Living Water is the Holy Spirit. Those who trust in Jesus have the promise of the indwelling of the Holy Spirit. Those who are baptized have the promise of being a child of God. God have provided you with water in your journey. His promise and His presence will strengthen you as you make the arduous trek out of the canyon.

There are other things that I put in my backpack. I make sure I have a couple extra pairs of socks. In my three trips across the canyon, I never had a blister. I credit that to the fact that I changed my socks at different points of the hike. Wet socks are breeding grounds for blisters. I also make sure that I have energy for the hike. Energy bars, energy chews, and fruit are my sources of choice. I usually will eat one at each break. It was important to keep my body hydrated and energized before I felt the need. When I felt the need, it may be too late or you will need to take an extended stop to make sure that my body was ready to go.

The application is this. God has provided you for what you need in the journey. The problem is that grief can cause you to isolate yourself and cut yourself off from what God has given you to face this challenge. Any way that you look at it, grief is an uphill and painful journey. Make sure that you use what has been given to you to avoid some of the added difficulties that may result.

I also bring some emergency items: first aid kit, whistle, flashlight, glow stick, and a cooling towel. I have used the flashlight, glow stick, and cooling towel, but fortunately, I did not have the need of first aid.

As stated earlier, God has given you tools to sustain you. He has given you His word. He has given you the Church. He has given you Himself. He also has given you tools for when you get hurt, among them the promise of forgiveness and restoration.

One more important "thing" I always had and always will have is a hiking partner. It is foolish to try to do this hike by yourself even though it is a well-travelled trail. The same is true in your grief journey. Don't try to go it alone.

Prayer — Lord, help me as I come out of the canyon. Help me to keep my focus and not lose hope. You are with me every step of the way. You have also given me gifts to strengthen me and encourage me. Help me to lean on my family and friends that you have given me. In Jesus' name, amen.

Scripture Readings for Day 15:

Isaiah 42

Behold my servant, whom I uphold,
    my chosen, in whom my soul delights;
I have put my Spirit upon him;
    he will bring forth justice to the nations.
He will not cry aloud or lift up his voice,
    or make it heard in the street;
a bruised reed he will not break,
    and a faintly burning wick he will not quench;
    he will faithfully bring forth justice.

Crushed

You can't tell as I walk by what is going on inside.
You can't see from outside what's been denied.
I smile and I laugh and try to carry on.
But a very important part of me is gone.
Each day I start without the one I love so much.
Each day I begin knowing that my heart is crushed.

Chorus
You said that a bruised reed you would not break.
That a weak wick you would not blow out.
You promised to be faithful to the end.
Lord, that's the promise I call out.
Where are you when I fall to the ground?
Where are you when I can't be found?
Where are you when darkness fills my soul?
Where are you when I lose control?

I try to live like things are normal.
I try to do what needs to be done.
I try to make all of my appointments.
I try to make it look like life is fun.
If I look a little frazzled and in a rush.
I'm trying to make it but my spirit's crushed.

You come to the broken hearted.
You come to the shattered soul.
With care you wrap what is fractured.
This cracked clay jar you have made whole.
You come to give the troubled rest.
You come to give hope in tempest.
You come to me and I am blessed.

Day 15
Crushed
Isaiah 42:1-3

Rather than broken or shattered, I think that crushed is a better way to describe how the person who is grieving feels. When something is broken or shattered, people can see it. When something is crushed or bruised, it looks normal from the outside. The problem is what is what is going on in the inside. I think about the times that unknowingly I have bitten into a bruised apple. I wish I could have seen my face. I would have seen my reaction and the revulsion were immediate. My face would be contorted.

As you go through your grief, you do the things that you normally do. I'm not talking just about your chores at home, going to work, and other daily routines. I'm talking about how people see you. They see you smile. They hear you laugh. They hear your voice, and it sounds like everything is okay. That is all on the outside.

If people could see inside, they would see the hole that is in your heart. They would see that your spirit is crushed. They would see that your soul is wounded as so many questions and emotions are crying out for attention. They would understand a little better why you are a little off. They would understand why you aren't acting yourself.

The hope and the promise that we have is that God sees. God who sees neither sleeps nor slumbers. God does not build a hedge around you to protect you from all hurt and pain. He tells you that there is a time to live and a time to die. There is a time to laugh and a time to cry. This time of pain has a purpose. Although the hole that this death has made cannot and will not ever be filled, it will not define who you are and how you live your life. Because life if defined by the Lord of life, who sees you and comes to you.

There is a great promise that God spoke through Isaiah, "a bruised reed he will not break. A weak flame he will not quench." At times, you may feel like your body is covered with bruises and your light is about to blow out. It is for that moment Jesus came. It is for that reason Jesus came. It is for that reason that you are invited to cast our cares on God, because he cares for you. It is for that reason, Jesus invites those who are weary and heavy laden to be yoked with him and to learn from him. When you feel like this, God wants you to know that he is with you, not to condemn but to lift you up.

The amazing thing is that God will use this time so you can help others who are going through something similar. I am not the only person who has grieved. You are not the only person who will grieve. But we are the ones who are grieving now. God will comfort us and will get us through this, so that we can comfort others with the same comfort that God gave us when our bodies, our spirits, and our souls felt crushed (2 Corinthians 1:3-7).

Prayer — Dear Lord, my heart, my soul, my spirit are all crushed. I don't have the strength to stand before You, so I cry out to You. Create in me a clean heart, a heart restored through You. Renew a right spirit within me. My spirit now is broken and only You can fix it. Restore to me the joy of Your salvation. Help me to tolerate this life at first and enjoy my life as time goes on. Please be present and let me know Your presence, for You uphold me with Your spirit. In Jesus' name. Amen

Scripture Readings for Day 16:

Psalm 31

Be gracious to me, O LORD, for I am in distress;
    my eye is wasted from grief;
    my soul and my body also.
For my life is spent with sorrow,
    and my years with sighing;
my strength fails because of my iniquity,
    and my bones waste away.
Because of all my adversaries I have become a reproach,
    especially to my neighbors,
and an object of dread to my acquaintances;
    those who see me in the street flee from me.
I have been forgotten like one who is dead;
    I have become like a broken vessel.
For I hear the whispering of many—
    terror on every side!—
as they scheme together against me,
    as they plot to take my life.
But I trust in you, O LORD;
    I say, "You are my God."
My times are in your hand;
    rescue me from the hand of my enemies
    and from my persecutors!
Make your face shine on your servant;
    save me in your steadfast love!

1 Thessalonians 4:

But we do not want you to be uninformed, brothers, about those who are asleep, that you may not grieve as others do who have no hope. For since we believe that Jesus died and rose again, even so, through Jesus, God will bring with him those who have fallen asleep.

Bad Grief

This is supposed to be a time of healing.
This is supposed to be when I learn to move on.
This is supposed to be a time of feeling
Like I have the strength to start to go on.
It's not a time of healing, but one of festering.
I'm not in control, and I'm not mastering.
I'm on my knees, pleading for relief.
Lord, deliver me from this bad, bad grief.

O Lord, when will this season come to an end?
I've been struggling much too long, and I can't take it.
There's only so much that I can stand while I bend
Before I snap. I don't know if I'll make it.
Your promises I hold dear. They are ever so near.
I hold them ever so tight and with all of my might.
I hope they bring peace, a calm, ever so brief.
Lord, deliver me from this bad, bad grief.

It's taken control, and I'm just muddling through.
I'm not thinking things out, not doing what I should do.
I'm closing myself off from the ones who want to help me.
I'm closing myself in. Though they try, can't get to me.
I'm losing touch, and I'm shaking like a leaf.
Lord, deliver me from this bad, bad grief.

In small, small ways You show me You are near.
In that still, small voice, You whisper in my ear.
The smile of my son tells me that I am loved.
A phone call from a friend shows that I'm loved.
A letter in the mail helps me know that I am loved.
Someone prayed with me, good to know that I am loved.
Still on my knees, still praying for relief.
Lord, change this all to a good, good grief.

Day 16
Bad Grief
Psalm 31:9-16, 1 Thessalonians 4:13, 14

Not long ago I had a conversation with a friend who had lost two siblings over a short span of time. She also mentioned that it took a couple of years to deal with these significant losses. I told her about the loss of my wife. I made the comment that I hadn't dealt with my grief very well. Insightfully, she responded, "Is there a wrong way to grieve?" I responded, "I didn't. I looked after my son and the church, but I didn't look after myself."

Grief is a natural phase after someone loses a loved one. Even more importantly, it is a gift of God given to help a person to deal with the death of someone that was loved dearly and to learn how to go forward without that person in it. Grief is to help heal when a person has been hurt more deeply than it was ever thought possible.

There is not one "right" way to grieve. There is not one right time frame in which it is appropriate to grieve. There is not a universal step by step program to use after a loved one has died. Each person is different. Each person who died was unique. Each relationship is one of a kind. The most important this is to feel the grief, to experience it. It cannot be avoided or circumvented. The consequence of not grieving is bad grief, or, as the professionals call it, complicated grief. Grief needs to be dealt with. It needs to be taken by the horns and ridden, no matter how difficult it may be at times.

There are distractions along the way that can hijack grief. A couple of those distractions for me were my son and my calling as a pastor. I thought it was admirable that I wanted to keep my son happy, but in so doing I deprived us both of grieving in a timely manner. Both of our lives were turned on their heads. Both of us lost a wonderful and amazing lady, his mother and my wife. She was worth crying over. She was worth grieving. But he was a happy boy and I wanted to help keep him that way. I did a good job of it. From my point of view, it caught up with me. I wonder when some day it will catch up with him.

Work was another barrier to grieving. I used my faith and my calling as a pastor to avoid dealing with grief. It was convenient and it made me look like an awfully strong man. I had lost my wife and was called to be the sole parent for my son. What a testament I was to those in the church and those who knew me. I talked about the confidence I had in the resurrection and the confidence that I had that she was with the Lord now.

But we were hurting. We had lost an important person in our lives. Now was the time to crawl into the lap of the eternal God and cry our eyes out. Now was the time for Marco and me to tell our God that He alone could give us the strength. I could not trust my own strength, neither could Marco. Now was the time to be encouraged and lifted up by the brothers and sisters in faith. Instead of doing that, I put on the front of being strong.

Paul tells us that we do not grieve like those who have no hope. He does not tell that we do not grieve. When have lost someone that we love, we need to get ready to grieve. It is the price and the reward for having loved someone deeply. It is the cost of someone having a great impact on a life. It will be bumpy. It will hurt deeply at times. In the end, we will be stronger people. But it is not a time for a brave face and for platitudes.

Prayer — Lord, this is the most painful time in my life. I lost someone who was so important to me. Give me the strength to walk through this time of loss. Don't let me avoid it. Give me the strength to deal with it and to learn from it. In Jesus' name. Amen

Scripture Readings for Day 17:

Psalm 107:10-16

Some sat in darkness and in the shadow of death,
    prisoners in affliction and in irons,
for they had rebelled against the words of God,
    and spurned the counsel of the Most High.
So he bowed their hearts down with hard labor;
    they fell down, with none to help.
Then they cried to the LORD in their trouble,
    and he delivered them from their distress.
He brought them out of darkness and the shadow of death,
    and burst their bonds apart.
Let them thank the LORD for his steadfast love,
    for his wondrous works to the children of man!
For he shatters the doors of bronze
    and cuts in two the bars of iron.

Matthew 10

And do not fear those who kill the body but cannot kill the soul. Rather fear him who can destroy both soul and body in hell. Are not two sparrows sold for a penny? And not one of them will fall to the ground apart from your Father. But even the hairs of your head are all numbered.

1 Peter 5

Humble yourselves, therefore, under the mighty hand of God so that at the proper time he may exalt you, casting all your anxieties on him, because he cares for you.

In the chains that I've forged

Locked up in a dungeon, a life full of misery.
The guards are watching over me.
Their names are pain, despair, and guilt.
The chains that hold me are ones I built.
I locked myself up, threw away the key.
Blind to what was going on in front of me.
Oh, these chains. Oh, these chains.

Chorus
I'm living in the chains that I've forged.
Each one I thoughtlessly made.
I'm living in the chains that I've forged
They're holding a life decayed.
That life had hope. That life had joy.
That life had life. That life had love.
That life would take any challenge on.
That life is now just hanging on.
As it hangs in the chains that I forged.

I'm looking at these links. I see what has put me here.
These chains have been made by my fear.
Each link, I see it bears a name.
Isolation, Pity, Guilt, and Shame.
Depression kept me up half the night.
Indecision kept its grip so tight.
Oh these chains, oh these chains.

But there's been a prison break.
A man has come and set me free.
He's told the guards to let me be.
Opened up the doors in front of me.
Broken each chain, sweet liberty.
He's broken the chains that I've forged.
Each one gently taken away.
He's broken the chains that I've forged.
At last I see the light of day.
No more chains, no more chains.

Day 17
The Chains I've Forged
Psalm 107:10-16, Matthew 10:28-30, 1 Peter 5:6-7

I used to watch Christmas specials every year during the weeks before Christmas day. There were certain movies that I had to see. One of them was the musical, *A Christmas Carol*. When I was young, Jacob Marley scared me. As I grew up, he was not as intimidating. But there is line that haunted me and still haunts me. When Jacob Marley came to visit his old business partner, he was covered with chains. When Ebenezer Scrooge asks him about the chains, Marley responds, "I wear the chains I forged in life. I made it link by link, and yard by yard. I girded it on of my own free will, and of my own free will I wore it."

One of the dangers of grief gone badly is that you don't deal with or resolve the triggers that warn you that you are going in a bad direction. The result is a weight on your body and soul. It is as though you are starting to have a chain put on you which saps both body and soul of strength.

Some of those triggers are physical, such as change in sleep patterns, change in diet, and a change in behavior. Some of the triggers are emotional, loss of joy and peace, loss of motivation and direction, increased anxiety, depression, to name a few.

Each of these complications is like a link in a chain. Each link weighed me down. I didn't recognize this in time or I didn't deal with it in time. Either way, the consequences of this inactivity on my part came with its results. My spirit was weighed down. My will was unable to move to decide the most basic functions. My body felt oppressed and sapped of energy.

All the while there was God's invitation waiting to be heeded. In Matthew 10:28-30, Jesus invited me, who was weak and heavy laden to come to him. Jesus promised to hook Himself up to my struggle. He promised to walk with me so I can learn from Him. Many times people push God away during the difficulty because they blame God for what is happening. God is my strongest link and He promises to be with me during this difficult time.

Another invitation is given in 1 Peter 5:6-7. With this invitation, God encourages us to give up trying to do this by ourselves and hand it over to Him. The reason that God makes this invitation is simple. He cares for me. God does not want me to struggle in this way. In the following verses, another reason is stated. There is someone in the background who wants to see my destruction. The devil is there like a lion ready to pounce on me. When I am in those chains, I am easy prey.

One by one, bring those links of the chain to God. One by one, God will lift the weight and lift the pain. One by one God will bring relief and the freedom that comes as the links are removed. Be confident of this, if the Son sets you free you will be free indeed.

Prayer — O Lord, I feel like a prisoner to the consequences of grief. At times, I don't have the strength to do anything but just to survive. I bring it all to You. I come to You weak and heavy laden. I cast my cares on You. Help me learn from You while You change my life and restore to me the life You have called me to live. Help me to share this hope with those who are struggling, o You God of all comfort. In Jesus' name, amen.

Scripture Readings for Day 18:

Nehemiah 8

Then he said to them, "Go your way. Eat the fat and drink sweet wine and send portions to anyone who has nothing ready, for this day is holy to our Lord. And do not be grieved, for the joy of the LORD is your strength."

Psalm 30

I will extol you, O LORD, for you have drawn me up
    and have not let my foes rejoice over me.
O LORD my God, I cried to you for help,
    and you have healed me.
O LORD, you have brought up my soul from Sheol;
    you restored me to life
    from among those who go down to the pit.
Sing praises to the LORD, O you his saints,
    and give thanks to his holy name.
For his anger is but for a moment,
    and his favor is for a lifetime.
Weeping may tarry for the night,
    but joy comes with the morning.
As for me, I said in my prosperity,
    "I shall never be moved."
By your favor, O LORD,
    you made my mountain stand strong;
you hid your face;
    I was dismayed.
To you, O LORD, I cry,
    and to the Lord I plead for mercy:
"What profit is there in my death,
    if I go down to the pit?
Will the dust praise you?
    Will it tell of your faithfulness?
Hear, O LORD, and be merciful to me!
    O LORD, be my helper!"
You have turned for me my mourning into dancing;
    you have loosed my sackcloth
    and clothed me with gladness,
that my glory may sing your praise and not be silent.
    O LORD my God, I will give thanks to you forever!

Where is the joy?

A new day, a new beginning
It's time to move from the past.
The ghosts were left miles behind.
Let's hope for a joy that will last.
But peace is so elusive
And the joy is so hard to find.
Searching for consolation
Anything that will ease my mind.

Chorus
So where is the joy?
They say the joy of the Lord is my strength.
And that joy will come in the morning.
But tears are my steady diet.
The night voices won't stay quiet.
And depression comes on without warning.
Where is the joy?

How sad is joy disappointed.
A promise that never materialized
Instead of a great turnaround,
Is an underdog unrealized.
Where the weight of stress takes its toll
Sleepless nights rob my resolve.
And all my attempts fall too short.
There's no answer this problem to solve.

There is the joy!
So yes, the joy of the Lord is my strength
And joy does come in the morning.
When I believe the things God has said
And I plant them firmly in my head.
I'm sending my fears a warning.

There is the joy.
There is the joy!
So yes, the joy of the Lord is my strength
And joy does come in the morning.
It's right there on my son's face
With each and every warm embrace
I'm sending my fears a warning.
There is the joy.

Day 18
Where is the joy?
Nehemiah 8:10, Psalm 30

Laughter is a great blessing and a fantastic cleansing agent. But in the early stages of grief, though there may be moments of laughter, there is no joy. At first, the pain of the loss is engulfing. Your life and your world have changed. At the best, you can be happy and laugh for a short time. Then the reality of your changed life returns. The foundation of your life has been shaken to the ground.

This is the reality. There is nothing wrong with you. There is nothing lacking in your faith or your trust in God. The person that you loved is gone. The person who has impacted your life in a profound manner will no longer be involved in your everyday life. All that remains are the memories. Joy may come in the future, but this is the season of mourning.

If you grieve, if you embrace the pain and the suffering, then over time joy will return. If you fail to embrace it, it will return after a much longer time. There is nothing wrong with how you are dealing with loss. What is "wrong" with you is the life has changed and you are searching for balance after the love of your life is gone.

There is something that you need to understand about joy. Joy is not a feeling. Joy is a state of being. You have joy not because the things in life are lining up as you planned or as you wished. You have joy because you know that something or Someone is bigger than the things that are happening all around you. You have joy because that Someone who is bigger than you is with you and is there to help. You have joy because the One who is with you is bigger than your pain, your sorrow, and your hurt. You have joy because you know that your pain and your hurt are tools to let you know the depth, the width, the height of God's love for you. In all things, you are more than a conqueror. You have joy not because of the situation. You have joy because God is always with you, no matter what the situation.

Prayer — O Lord, at the times that joy is elusive and all I can see and feel is pain, help me to know that You are with me. Help me to know that though now is the time of sorrow, joy comes in the morning. Help me to know that after this struggle, I will be able to support and encourage others who are struggling through their loss of a loved one. In Jesus' name, amen

Scripture Readings for Day 19:

Psalm 139

O LORD, you have searched me and known me!
You know when I sit down and when I rise up;
  you discern my thoughts from afar.
You search out my path and my lying down
  and are acquainted with all my ways.
Even before a word is on my tongue,
  behold, O LORD, you know it altogether.
You hem me in, behind and before,
  and lay your hand upon me.
Such knowledge is too wonderful for me;
  it is high; I cannot attain it.
Where shall I go from your Spirit?
  Or where shall I flee from your presence?
If I ascend to heaven, you are there!
  If I make my bed in Sheol, you are there!
If I take the wings of the morning
  and dwell in the uttermost parts of the sea,
even there your hand shall lead me,
  and your right hand shall hold me.
If I say, "Surely the darkness shall cover me,
  and the light about me be night,"
even the darkness is not dark to you;
  the night is bright as the day,
  for darkness is as light with you.

Isaiah 43:1-2

But now thus says the LORD,
    he who created you, O Jacob,
    he who formed you, O Israel:
"Fear not, for I have redeemed you;
    I have called you by name, you are mine.
When you pass through the waters, I will be with you;
    and through the rivers, they shall not overwhelm you;
when you walk through fire you shall not be burned,
    and the flame shall not consume you.

Where Are You?

You promised to be with Your people.
You promised to be with me.
You promised You'd never leave.
I've looked around. Where could You be?
I feel forgotten, mistaken.
Like You've fallen asleep.
Like You are not listening
When I pray my soul to keep.

Where are You, Lord?
I'm running out of hope.
Where are You, Lord?
It's hard just to cope.
Where are You Lord?
I'm trusting in Your grace.
Where are You Lord?
I'm in Your Holy Place.

I'm walking through the valley
Limping in this vale of tears.
Not seeing any relief in sight
Struggling with doubts and fears.
Looking for the shepherd
To take me in his arms.
His rod and staff to comfort
To deliver me from harm.

When I'm looking at the problems
That is all I see.
When I look at the solution
I know You are with me.
When I hear the voice of turmoil
That is all I hear.
When I hear the voice of comfort
I know that You are near.

Where am I child?
I'm here right by your side?
Where am I child?
I'm here to be your guide.
In your friends, in their face,
In every caring embrace,
In your child, in that smile,
In each prayer across the mile.
I am here, I AM here.

Day 19
Where are you?
Psalm 139:7-12; Isaiah 43:1, 2

Nobody likes to feel alone. That awkward time in the store comes, when after looking intently at a pair of shoes, you look up and wonder where your child went. Panic fills your mind and your heart starts racing. It is increased when your child experiences the same thing. The question that both of you ask is, "Where are you?"

That question will be directed at God a few times during your grief journey. Like Mary and Martha, you may say to God, "if you had been here, my (brother) would not have died." Although you know that the hour of death awaits all, you are never ready for the moment when the time comes. You focus so much on the loss and the pain that you think that you are alone at the time. You think that God has abandoned you and left you to go through this time alone.

God does have an answer for you. "I was with the one you loved and I was with you." God's promise is that precious in his sight is the death of his saints (Psalm 116:15). The promise that Jesus gave to Mary and Martha is the promise that I hold dear. "I am the resurrection and the life. Whoever believes in me, though he die, yet will he live." This promise was made not only to me but to everyone who trusts in Jesus. My wife is with Jesus. Jesus was also there with me to get through the trauma of the moment.

The question continues in the days, the weeks, and the months that follow. There are times that you feel like you are feeling this pain all by yourself. Sometimes you feel like the promises of God are not being realized. Sometimes you feel like you don't have the strength to go on. You feel like God has abandoned you. So you raise the question, "where are you God?"

The answer is the same. God is with you.

Many times I did not see that presence because of my focus. I focused on the problem. I focused on my hurt and loss. I focused on who

I no longer had. I did not keep my eyes on Jesus. I did not trust in God's promises. I did not see Him as he worked through the lives of the people that He brought into my life.

Maybe you don't see God at work in your life because you have a false understanding of how God is at work in your life. God is there to work with you through the hardship, not to remove the hardship. God is there. He is fighting for you. He is sending reinforcements. He is comforting and encouraging you. No matter how dark or desperate the situation, be certain of this. God is with you.

Prayer — O Lord, sometimes when I look around, all I see is the problem. All I see is the pain and what I no longer have. Help me to hold on to you. Help me to trust your promises. Help me to see you in the lives of those who come to help me. Help me to see that you are there to give me strength, comfort, and encouragement. In Jesus' name. Amen

Scripture Readings for Day 20:

Proverbs 7

My son, keep my words
    and treasure up my commandments with you;
keep my commandments and live;
    keep my teaching as the apple of your eye;
bind them on your fingers;
    write them on the tablet of your heart.
Say to wisdom, "You are my sister,"
    and call insight your intimate friend,

Proverbs 27

Faithful are the wounds of a friend;
    profuse are the kisses of an enemy.

Oil and perfume make the heart glad,
    and the sweetness of a friend comes from his earnest counsel.

I hear You in her voice

I hear You in her voice.
Her voice brings me a calm.
It led me through the wilderness.
To my shattered heart, a balm.
She called me to your throne,
Where your promises are true.
"You've got this Steve." Just believe.
His strength will see you through.

I hear You in her voice.
Her voice tells me that I'm loved.
At times, I didn't love myself.
But she set my sights above.
She reminded me of who I am,
A servant of our Lord.
"Steve, you are incredible."
And great things are in store.

I hear you in her voice.
Her voice fills me with cheer.
When laughter was a distant thought,
A smile did reappear.
She is a gift of God,
Who prayed me through the pit.
She walked me through the wilderness.
"Steve, you will get through it."

Your voice reassures me.   Your voice always leads me.
Your voice does remind me.   Your voice with hope feeds me.
Your voice brings me comfort.   Your voice brings me peace.
Your voice gives direction.   Your voice will not cease.

Day 20
I hear you in her voice
Proverbs 7:1-4, 27:6 and 9

One of the temptations when one is grieving is to isolate oneself. It is one of those irrational things that I did. A major reason for my coming back to Michigan was that I was moving closer to family. I did not take advantage of it. There were a couple of times we were going to be with family for Easter and a Graduation party. But either Marco or I was sick. I went to visit my parents in July and I realized that this was the first time that I had visited with them in seven months. Not only did I not get together with my parents, I did not get together with most of my family. I had a wonderful built in support system but I did not make use of it.

I did not keep in contact with my friends, either. There was only one person that I did talk with, and she was my only support system. Her name is Cher. When I needed help the most, she was the type of friend that everybody needs. She was compassionate and sympathetic. She understood the complexity of my grief and identified with my experience. She was articulate. She was able to express God's grace in a manner appropriate with what I was going through and brought me comfort. She was an encourager. She didn't give up on me. She was for me what Christians are called to be to one another. She lifted me up. She comforted me with the grace of God. She encouraged me with the Gospel. She lifted me up in prayer. I will always thank God for Cher and how she helped me.

As I said, I pray that you all have somebody like Cher in your life. She was God's gift to me during this time. She was God's light which led me out of the deep darkness of grief and depression.

At times, you may feel like you are by yourself. If you are at that point and you feel like you have shut yourself off from those that God has put in your life, like I did, understand this. There are people that God has given you. They are gifts who will bring the grace and the promises of God to you in a way that you cannot imagine. Each friend will encourage you but in a unique way that nobody else can. They are God's voice sharing his message of hope.

Prayer — O Lord, You have promised not to leave me alone. You are with me through the friends that You give me. Lord, please give them wisdom to share Your thoughts in my time of weakness. Give them sympathy and compassion to share Your heart with me. Give them courage to encourage me with Your promises. Give me humility to hear You speak to me through the people that You bring into my life. In Jesus' name, amen.

Scripture Readings for Day 21:

Psalm 22

"He trusts in the Lord; let him deliver him;
 let him rescue him, for he delights in him!"

Matthew 5

"You are the salt of the earth, but if salt has lost its taste, how shall its saltiness be restored? It is no longer good for anything except to be thrown out and trampled under people's feet.

"You are the light of the world. A city set on a hill cannot be hidden. Nor do people light a lamp and put it under a basket, but on a stand, and it gives light to all in the house. In the same way, let your light shine before others, so that they may see your good works and give glory to your Father who is in heaven.

Ephesians 2

For we are his workmanship, created in Christ Jesus for good works, which God prepared beforehand, that we should walk in them.

What Have I Become?

When I look into the mirror I wonder
Who's that looking back at me?
It once had joy. That face once smiled
Now apathy looks back at me.
There's no twinkle in the eye.
Just a blank and empty stare.
No sign of hope or joy at all
A life that just doesn't care.
Chorus

Oh, what have I become?
A burned out shell and an empty case.
Oh what have I become?
A victim of life searching for grace.
How can this be undone?
Not by myself and I need a hand.
How can this be undone?
Stop building your house on top of sand.

When I look in my son's eyes I wonder.
I wonder what he sees in me.
Does he see pain? Does he see joy?
Or does he see sweet victory?
Are my life and words coherent?
Does it match the words that I say?
As I struggle with her death and my life,
I hope he sees joy wins the day.

In a still small voice, I hear God say.
This is who you are.
You are my child. The apple of my eye.
You are my son. The salt and the light.
My handiwork, my sheep.
You are an heir. You are my witness.
You're a promise that I keep.
This is who you are.

Day 21
What have I become?
Psalm 22:8, Matthew 5:13-16, Ephesians 2:10

This is not the prayer of one who is grieving normally. This is the prayer of one who has not grieved and was caught unaware by grief. This is the prayer of one who has come to realize that his life has fallen apart over the last few months and did not even realize it.

Then came the moment of realization. What was obvious to everybody has become a moment of revelation. The sad part is that by now the person was so entrenched in bad habits that had crippled him that it was difficult to get back to the way you used to be.

This moment of realization is a very difficult one. For me, my sense of self-worth was at an all-time low. There was very little good that I saw in myself and the life that I was living.

That is where I stayed for too long and went further down in grief towards depression. The problem was my focus was on yourself. I had many red flags when I was sinking down in my grief. I was not getting enough sleep. As a result, I was not functioning in my job as well as I should have been. I did not have a lot of energy because of sleep deprivation as well as my emotional state. I was not thinking properly. I started to criticize myself because I was not acting like I used to act. I could not make decisions. I gave myself plenty of material to critique.

There was one benefit from this self-criticism. It helped me to recognize that I had a problem. It took me a while after this realization to do something to make myself better. I wish I would have realized this and acted on that realization much earlier.

The best thing you can do is to take your focus off yourself. There are many more productive ways to spend your time thinking. Think about the people that God has placed in your life. You are to be a blessing to these people. You probably want to be a blessing to these people, at least most of them. Think about your job and the people with whom you work. God gave you special talents to perform that job.

Think about the impact that your life can make in the lives of people within your sphere of influence.

More importantly, think of what God did for you and what God thinks of you. God loved each of us so much that He gave His only son, so that everyone who believes in Him should not die but have everlasting life. That everlasting life will be lived with the God who gave His son. God wants to spend eternity with you and with me. Think of what God did for you. No greater love has a man than this that he lay down his life for his friends. The Father gave up His Son and His Son gave up His life. God's love for you is undeniable. You are loved by God. You are treasured by Him. He has called you to be his child. He promises to be with you.

Furthermore, look at how the titles that God uses for you reflect His love for you and the value that He places on you. You are a child of God and an heir. You are His workmanship. You are His ambassador. You are a chosen people. You are sheep of His pasture. He has loved you with an everlasting love. He is preparing a place for you in His house. I pray that this is your focus when you doubt your value and God's plan for you.

Prayer — Sometimes when I look at myself, I only see my short comings and my failures. Help me to see myself the way that You see me. Help me to see that You have covered me with the blood of Jesus, so when You see me You see Your son. Help me see that I am a blessing so that others may be blessed by You through me. You have written my name on the palm of Your hand. Thank You for that great love and help me to honor Your love for me. In Jesus' name, amen.

Scripture Readings for Day 22:

Psalm 103

Bless the LORD, O my soul,
    and all that is within me,
    bless his holy name!
Bless the LORD, O my soul,
    and forget not all his benefits,
who forgives all your iniquity,
    who heals all your diseases,
who redeems your life from the pit,
    who crowns you with steadfast love and mercy,
who satisfies you with good
    so that your youth is renewed like the eagle's.
The LORD works righteousness
    and justice for all who are oppressed.
He made known his ways to Moses,
    his acts to the people of Israel.
The LORD is merciful and gracious,
    slow to anger and abounding in steadfast love.
He will not always chide,
    nor will he keep his anger forever.
He does not deal with us according to our sins,
    nor repay us according to our iniquities.
For as high as the heavens are above the earth,
    so great is his steadfast love toward those who fear him;
as far as the east is from the west,
    so far does he remove our transgressions from us.
As a father shows compassion to his children,
    so the LORD shows compassion to those who fear him.
For he knows our frame;
    he remembers that we are dust.

I'm just a man

Psalm 103:14

I'm just a man. I can only bear so much
I'm lost. I'm scared. And I'm losing touch.
"I don't know how you do it."
They say time and time again.
It brings no consolation.
It reminds me of the pain.

Chorus
I'm just a man, a mortal nothing more.
But I look to God, who I worship and adore.
He is my strength, my fortress and my shield.
In him is my trust, to whom I will always yield.

I'm just a man. Oh, what more can I take?
My love is gone and know my life's at stake.
And no, that was not enough.
I also lost direction.
I wake up and I wonder,
"Oh, where is your protection?"

I'm just a man. You ask too much of me.
With all I've lost, oh, just let me lie.
I am at my wits end.
I've tried all that I can do.
But it is never enough.
I hope for a life that's new.

Day 22

I'm Just a Man

Psalm 103:14

"Lord, I'm just a man. I can only take so much." I remember praying this prayer. It was a Sunday afternoon. My sleep problems returned. My facade was down. I went to church, and everyone could see my sad state. I remember somebody saying, "You have always been so strong." I was not strong that day. I prayed to God and told Him that He had pushed me far enough. "Lord, I'm just a man. I don't think that I can take any more." It was that night that I vowed that I am going to use these sleepless nights productively and write the titles for these poems.

You may be reading this book because you are at your breaking point. I encourage you to pray this prayer. "Lord, I am just a man. Help me." When you pray it, I hope that you mean it. I hope that you understand that there will be consequences to this prayer. In some way, God will answer that prayer.

You ask two important things as you pray this way. First and most important, you are not able to get out this place you are in all by yourself. If you are like me, you tried to be strong and independent far too long. You thought that by your faith, not by God's help, you could plow through this. You finally realized that this is not possible. Secondly and most importantly, God can do all things. Think of all the impossible things that God did in the Bible. A ninety-year old gave birth to a son. A nation marched across the Red Sea on dry land, and an ensuing army drowned in that same sea. A man survived three days in a great fish. Three young men were thrown into a furnace and did not get burned. A man survived a night in the lion den. A conquered nation returned to their homeland without a fight. A virgin conceived and gave birth to a son. A man was crucified and came to life after three days. We are praying to the God who will do great things for His people.

88

Another thing that you need to know is that God has made us to be more than just a man, more than just a pile of dust. God has worked in us in many ways. We are called, justified, glorified, loved, redeemed, blessed, restored, and sanctified. God sees us as chosen, royal, precious, special, beloved, holy, forgiven, reconciled, and righteous.

At this very low point in life, it is important to see yourself the way that God sees you. He sees you as His child. He sees you as one who has been clothed in Christ. He sees you as an heir of His kingdom. This trial will pass but His love and commitment to you is eternal.

Prayer — At times, I feel so weak. Help me to put my trust in You and to believe that You will be with me when I go through this difficult time. I may think that I am only dust, but You see me as Your child. You put Your name on me in my baptism. You promised to be with me always. Help me to trust in these promises. In Jesus' name, amen.

Scripture Readings for Day 23:

Ezekiel 34

For thus says the Lord GOD: Behold, I, I myself will search for my sheep and will seek them out. As a shepherd seeks out his flock when he is among his sheep that have been scattered, so will I seek out my sheep, and I will rescue them from all places where they have been scattered on a day of clouds and thick darkness. And I will bring them out from the peoples and gather them from the countries, and will bring them into their own land. And I will feed them on the mountains of Israel, by the ravines, and in all the inhabited places of the country. I will feed them with good pasture, and on the mountain heights of Israel shall be their grazing land. There they shall lie down in good grazing land, and on rich pasture they shall feed on the mountains of Israel. I myself will be the shepherd of my sheep, and I myself will make them lie down, declares the Lord GOD. I will seek the lost, and I will bring back the strayed, and I will bind up the injured, and I will strengthen the weak, and the fat and the strong I will destroy. I will feed them in justice.

Then I saw the Shepherd's Face

Ezekiel 34:11-16

Scared and afraid, I ran distracted.
Without thinking where I ran.
Not knowing about what was right or left.
No thought, without a plan.
And when I finally stopped and looked around.
Fear seized me. Would I be found?

Then I saw the Shepherd's face. I saw Your love, Your fear.
I saw the anguish of Your chase. Relieved the end was near.

You lifted me up on your broad shoulders.
I shook from fear and shame.
Your voice assured me. Truly all was well.
You called me by my name.
Fear melted to peace as you sang your song.
Your voice assured me, now nothing was wrong.

Then I saw the shepherd's face.   With him, I am at peace.
In his arms, a special place.   At long last, I am at ease.

The problems were far from being over.
The shepherd saw my pain.
He saw that I was hurt and so broken
I might never walk again.
Tenderly he dressed me. Aching day and night.
Patiently he sat by my side, holding me so tight.

Then I saw the Shepherd's face.   I knew what He would do.
He would not spare a single grace   To make my life like new.

He leads me to pastures green and quiet.
His rod and staff are near.

90

Through the valleys dark and dangerous
With Him, no need to fear.
The enemies, they may surround me.
By His side is where I will always be.

Then I see the shepherd's face.
A smile that will not end.
Disappointment? Not a trace.
A sure and constant friend.

The coyotes howl,
   the bears may growl.
The fox and coyote,
   near they may be.

The lions roar
   and the eagles soar.
You're between them and me
   so calm I'll be.

For I have seen the shepherd's face.
Those eyes are a warm embrace.

It's seen me through each trial.
And I love his precious smile.

Jesus,
lead thou on,
till our rest
is won.

Day 23

Then I Saw the Shepherd's Face

Ezekiel 34:11-16

One of the most beloved images in the Bible is that of God as the Shepherd. This image was so beautifully portrayed by David in the 23rd Psalm. At every funeral that I have ever attended, this psalm is read. Sometimes on the cover of the bulletin, there is a picture of a shepherd sitting under a tree near a pond or a river as the sheep graze on the green grass. Again, in the New Testament, Jesus states that he is the Good Shepherd. The sheep recognize the Shepherd's voice and will follow wherever He goes. The shepherd loves His sheep so much He is willing to die for them. These images have helped endear the image of shepherd in the Christian community.

Ezekiel does not portray the role of the shepherd in such a peaceful manner. Ezekiel has the shepherd out chasing after his beloved way-ward sheep. Although it is fitting, it was not complimentary for the Is-raelites and God's people to be called sheep.

Sheep can be stupid animals. They are easily frightened. They are easily distracted. So the shepherd has to find them when they are lost. The time that they are lost can be a scary time. They are separated from the flock, and they don't have the protection of the shepherd. I can only imagine the relief that comes to the sheep when it sees the shepherd come near who will take it back to safety. At times, we stray as well. Even though I held on to the promises of God, I strayed from God as I looked at the loss of my wife and all the responsibilities that were thrust on me, then at my failure to deal with it in a healthy manner. I started to listen to voices that led me away from the promises that I held on to. Yes, I held on to the promise, but I did not hold on to the One who made the promise. But the Lord sought me out. Although there was a lot of healing that needed to happen, what a comfort and joy to be in the grasp of the Shepherd.

That was the next image that Ezekiel gives me. The shepherd is also a veterinarian, who tends to the wounds of the sheep. My body is weak from the weight of stress and depression. My spirit is beaten up by me beating myself up, thinking that I should have known better and done better. My soul is wounded by the attacks of the voices that Satan has used to separate me from the Lord, my shepherd. As I look at the eyes of the Shepherd as he takes care of me. His eyes are full of love and compassion. There's a look of concern on His face as He deals with the wounds and He works at healing. There is only one thing the Shepherd wants and that is that His sheep gets better. I am that sheep. You are that sheep.

Prayer — O Lord, my Good Shepherd, thank You for not only looking for me when I was lost but finding me as well. Thank You for Your love and compassion in which You dealt with me, Your wounded sheep. Thank You for all that You do for me, Your stubborn sheep. In Jesus' name. Amen

Scripture Readings for Day 24:

Habakkuk 3

Though the fig tree should not blossom,
    nor fruit be on the vines,
the produce of the olive fail
    and the fields yield no food,
the flock be cut off from the fold
    and there be no herd in the stalls,
yet I will rejoice in the LORD;
    I will take joy in the God of my salvation.
GOD, the Lord, is my strength;
    he makes my feet like the deer's;
    he makes me tread on my high places.

I Choose Joy

Habakkuk 3:17-19

Life happened in ways I neither chose nor planned.
If I had my druthers, everything would be grand.
But that's not what has happened.
Now I am at my wits' end.
How will I deal with these troubles that annoy?
Will I choose frustration, or will I choose joy?

Chorus
I choose joy, for You walk with me.
I choose joy, for You talk with me.
I choose joy, for it makes me strong.
I choose joy, it helps me get along.
I choose joy, for it makes me sing.
I choose joy, in spite of everything.
I choose joy. I choose joy.

At times I'm a loser. At least that's how I feel.
Going through the motions. Nothing at all seems real.
I won't let that define me
Or make it all I see.
I have a certain confidence that I choose to employ
Holding on to promises and hanging on to joy.

Life is more peaceful when I see You in control
Though my heart is troubled, I know You guard my soul.
The troubles, they do abound
But by Your side I will be found.
Though life, it may seem hopeless. Please don't think me coy.
Now I say beyond a doubt, today, I choose joy.

Day 24
I Choose Joy
Habakkuk 3:17-19

I remember when I was growing up there were always reasons to be happy. When Michigan or one of my Detroit teams won a game, I was happy. When it was a sunny day, I was happy. When I got to play with my friends, I was happy. Even when bad things happened, I would find a reason to be happy. It was a rainy day. I was happy because I could read my Hardy Boys book. When I was sick, I was happy because I got to spend more time with Mom.

There is a difference between being happy and being joyful. Now, if I make it through the day and nothing bad happens, I am happy. I may not be joyful, though. I may think that it could have gone better. I may have had one of those days when nothing has gone right. But I thank God because He saw me through it, and I am now at home with my son.

Anybody can be happy, but not everybody is joyful. Being joyful is an attitude or a decision that one makes. It depends on who or what you want to make as your focus. As a child of God, I am joyful for so many reasons. No matter how many battles I may lose, I know that the war has already been won. I know that I am forgiven. I know that I am a child of God, and God's love will never end. I know that God is faithful.

In life, there is a lot of pain and a lot of heartache. There is also a lot of good. The question is on which will you focus? Are you going to choose to be a victim? Are you going to choose to dwell on the pain, the hardship, the sickness, the loss, the failure, or the things you don't have? If that is your focus, you may have times when you are happy but you are not going to know joy. If you choose to see yourself as the winner, you will be able to put those above problems in perspective. I am experiencing pain and loss now, but this is not who I am or where I'll stay. This trial is a tool to make me stronger. It is a venue to come closer to my God. It is an instrument to get rid of those things in my life that distract me from my Lord.

What I learn from this promise that God gave to Habakkuk is this. I won't let what I don't see distract me from what I have in God. I do not see the fruit of my labors. I don't have the comfort of a full stomach or a full bank account. But I am full. I am joyful. I am thankful. I am grateful. I am hopeful. I am cheerful. I am all these things because of who God is and what He does, has done and continues to do. I don't need to see these things because God has shown me who He is and what he Has done.

Prayer — Dear Lord, thank You for all that You have done. Even before I knew You, You did so much for me. You left behind a legacy of faithfulness to me and Your people. You demonstrated Your love not only with words but also with actions. You came to me and called me to be Your child. You promised to always be with me. You have always been faithful. That gives me strength when I face this trial. You will be with me. You will strengthen me. You will remind me of Your faithfulness. I, in turn, will keep my eyes on You, the author and perfecter of my faith. I will walk in joy for You are with me and will walk with me through this. In Jesus' name. Amen.

Scripture Readings for Day 25:

Haggai 2

In the seventh month, on the twenty-first day of the month, the word of the LORD came by the hand of Haggai the prophet, "Speak now to Zerubbabel the son of Shealtiel, governor of Judah, and to Joshua the son of Jehozadak, the high priest, and to all the remnant of the people, and say, 'Who is left among you who saw this house in its former glory? How do you see it now? Is it not as nothing in your eyes? Yet now be strong, O Zerubbabel, declares the LORD. Be strong, O Joshua, son of Jehozadak, the high priest. Be strong, all you people of the land, declares the LORD. Work, for I am with you, declares the LORD of hosts, according to the covenant that I made with you when you came out of Egypt. My Spirit remains in your midst. Fear not.

1 Peter 1:

Having purified your souls by your obedience to the truth for a sincere brotherly love, love one another earnestly from a pure heart, since you have been born again, not of perishable seed but of imperishable, through the living and abiding word of God; for

"All flesh is like grass
    and all its glory like the flower of grass.
The grass withers,
    and the flower falls,
but the word of the Lord remains forever."

And this word is the good news that was preached to you.

But You Remain

I'm walking through my house and see all the memories.
I see the signs of how of how my life used to be.
But every step I take, every glance I make is a reminder
Of all that I lost, all that was taken away.
Lord, I'm trying to make sense of this life I live.
I'm praying that You will have some hope to give.

Chorus
But You remain. When I have nothing else to hold on to.
You remain. When I have no one else to call out to.
You remain. When I have nothing else to stand on.
You remain. And You are what I need, and You remain.

I look at my life, and I see all the dreams unfulfilled,
The ones that can never become a reality.
This life is a shadow of the one I was supposed to live.
At times I wonder what else will be taken from me.
Lord, I'm hoping that soon I'll be led to Your light.
I'm praying that You'll step in and make it right.

Lo, I am with you. I remain.
I will be with you always. I remain.
I won't leave you desolate. I remain.
My comfort I give to you. I remain.
Immanuel, God is with us. I remain.
I will come to you. I remain.

Day 25
But You Remain
Haggai 2:1-5, 1 Peter 1:22-25

There is always just one hope. Sometimes that is more apparent than others. Before I realized that one hope, my focus was on what was going wrong. My focus was on the problem. All my energy was spent on worrying about the problem and focusing on the effects of the loss that I failed to realize that there was a solution, or better yet, the One who resolves and restores.

Over time, for me, the loss of my wife was all encompassing.

As long as your focus is on the problem, you are in a losing position. The problems multiply. This happens for a couple of reasons. As you focus on the problem, you start thinking of other problems and that raises more problems and more considerations of things to worry about. As a result of that, you worry. There are temptations that arise to appease worry, such as eating or drinking. Another result is to have trouble sleeping. During the night, you might watch programs that cause more problems yet. Or maybe, you might just lie in bed and never get back to sleep. This lack of sleep affects your everyday life. The snowball of worry grows.

The reality is this is where you will remain as long as you focus on the problem. There is a solution and there is a promise. They are interrelated. The solution lies in focusing your attention on the Lord of your salvation. The promise is that the Lord of your salvation promises to be with you.

There is a great comfort. It is the comfort that, no matter how much your life may change, how much may be taken from you, there is one thing that does not change. God is the same yesterday, today, and tomorrow. No matter how much your life has changed because someone or something was taken from you, God's word and His promise remain.

These promises address all that has changed in your life. These promises remind you that this life is short, but God is eternal and His word does not change. God's word remains and God commits Himself to those words of promise.

Those words are what I held onto with all my might and with all my strength during the time that my life seemed to be falling apart. I trusted that the God who made those promises would be faithful to His word. Here are a handful of the promises that brought me comfort.

"I am the resurrection and the life. Whoever believes in me, though he die, yet shall he live." John 11:25

"I will not leave you as orphans; I will come to you. " John 14:18

I have said these things to you, that in me you may have peace. In the world you will have tribulation. But take heart; I have overcome the world." John 16:33

"And we know that for those who love God all things work together for good, for those who are called according to his purpose." Romans 8:28

"He will wipe away every tear from their eyes, and death shall be no more, neither shall there be mourning, nor crying, nor pain anymore, for the former things have passed away." Revelation 21:4

Prayer — Thank You Lord that You are faithful to Your word and committed Yourself to the cause of Your people. No matter how much may change or how my life will never be the same, You are the same. Your word never changes. So my hope is constant, whatever the situation. In Jesus' name, amen.

Scripture Readings for Day 26:

1 Peter 5

Humble yourselves, therefore, under the mighty hand of God so that at the proper time he may exalt you, casting all your anxieties on him, because he cares for you. Be sober-minded; be watchful. Your adversary the devil prowls around like a roaring lion, seeking someone to devour. Resist him, firm in your faith, knowing that the same kinds of suffering are being experienced by your brotherhood throughout the world. And after you have suffered a little while, the God of all grace, who has called you to his eternal glory in Christ, will himself restore, confirm, strengthen, and establish you. To him be the dominion forever and ever. Amen.

Gonna Pray through This

Chorus
Gonna pray through this.
I'm holding on to the One who has a hold on me.
Gonna pray through this.
I'm looking to the One who's looking out for me.
Gonna pray through this.
I'm coming to the One who came after me.
Gonna pray through this.
I'm trusting the promises of him who promises.
Gonna pray through this. Gonna pray through this.

In an instant my life just changed
With no answer to the question why.
No way would my life be the same.
At first just a chore to get by.
Thank God for friends and family
Who stepped in at my time of need.
No, my strength did not come from within
My strength came when I was down on my knees

This void hasn't gotten any smaller.
It seems to linger and cloud each day.
The more time passes I realize
I lost my confidence along the way.
My thinking's hazy and clouded.
I don't trust the thoughts I think.
I've closed myself off from my friends.
Help me Lord, I'm on the brink.

And when I pray, my Lord hears my plea.
And when I pray, I know God is with me.
And when I pray, the Lord gives me peace.
And when I pray, there is a sweet release.
And when I pray, I rest in my Father's arms.
And when I pray, comes a calm from alarms.
Oh when I pray, Oh when I pray.
God is with me.

Day 26
Gonna pray through this
Psalm 116, 1 Peter 5:6-11

One of my favorite hymns is "What a Friend We Have in Jesus." The line "what a privilege to carry everything to God in prayer" is one of my favorite lyrics. When I consider it, I am truly humbled by the honor God grants us. The God of the universe promises to listen to me, a person in a small town in Michigan. The Lord of the Church invites me to come into his presence. If the Governor or even the President would grant me this honor, it would be all that I would be talking about for months. I would bring it up until the day I died. Yet every day, I come before my God, and He listens to me when I pray. What a privilege!

I remember saying the words, "I'm gonna pray through this" one of my sleepless nights. I began to apply the lessons I was learning and what I had always known. When my mind was racing, I began to recognize that these were the ways that Satan was using to distract me and drag me down. I wasn't going to let that continue.

My prayers became more specific. They addressed the concerns that were keeping me awake at night. They recognized that I was trying to handle all this by myself and putting them on my shoulders. My shoulders are not big enough. My help comes from the One who took all of this on his shoulders and gave His life for me.

One of my favorite promises of God is His gracious invitation to cast our cares (anxieties) on Him because He cares for us (2 Peter 5:7). Like my prayers, I took things out of context. When you reflect on this promise it is important to keep it in context. This is what I mean.

The promise begins with a call to humility. If you are like me, casting cares on God is a last resort. I try to suck it up and only ask for help as a last resort. Part of humility is to trust in God as a first resort. Asking for help is not a sign of weakness, but a sign of a strong character.

On the back end of the promise is a reminder of what is at stake. Satan is ready to pounce on any sign of weakness. Satan knows that when we listen to the anxieties in our lives we are not listening to God. He knows that when we are looking at our problems, our eyes are not fixed on Jesus. He knows that when we are burdened and heavy laden, we are weighed down and thinking about ourselves and the hurt, and not coming to our Lord to yoke Himself to us.

That is part of the beauty of prayer. Not only do we talk to God but He talks back if we take the time to listen. We look to the one who looks after us and we are reminded of the depth of His love and concern for us. We also unburden our minds and our souls knowing that He carries the weight for us.

Prayer — O Lord, thank You for listening to me. Thank You for Your loving concern. Thank You for freeing me of this burden. Thank You for the privilege to come to You in prayer, knowing that You listen and truly care about what is happening in my life. When I pray, help me to truly believe that You are the power of prayer. You are the one who brings me peace and gives me hope. In Jesus's name, Amen.

Scripture Readings for Day 27:

Malachi 3

Behold, I send my messenger, and he will prepare the way before me. And the Lord whom you seek will suddenly come to his temple; and the messenger of the covenant in whom you delight, behold, he is coming, says the LORD of hosts. But who can endure the day of his coming, and who can stand when he appears? For he is like a refiner's fire and like fullers' soap. **He will sit as a refiner and purifier of silver, and he will purify the sons of Levi and refine them like gold and silver, and they will bring offerings in righteousness to the LORD.** Then the offering of Judah and Jerusalem will be pleasing to the LORD as in the days of old and as in former years.

Your Reflection

Malachi 3:3

You picked me out like a silver nugget.
I was so happy to be in Your hands.
I was feeling blessed to be called Your child
And to be following all Your commands.
What joy to know that You had a plan
For the life of this very simple man.

Chorus
My life is in Your hands.
You're watching over me.
My life is purified by fire.
Your eye's on me constantly.
Removing every imperfection
Until You see Your reflection.

Had no idea what would happen next
My life would go through the hottest flame.
All around me, my life was burning up.
I knew my life would never be the same.
My only hope; I was in Your hands
I was trusting that You had a plan.

How would You know when the job was done?
How would You know when I'd be ready?
The flames are getting way too much for me.
Trusting, but enough's enough already.
The silver is starting to glow.
Your face is there and now You know.

Day 27
Your Reflection
Malachi 3:3

I have been intrigued by the imagery of the silversmith refining silver. I really never knew much about it. I figured it had something to do about getting rid of the impurities or the dross in the silver to make it a purer metal.

I have learned the following things about silver. First, as far as precious metals go, silver has a low melting point. Therefore, the silversmith has to be alert. If the silver is in the fire too long, it will be ruined.

Each person has a melting point. Some people can take more trial and hardship than others. At some point, everybody melts. At some point, the person will say to God during the time of trial and purification, enough is enough. There is comfort in knowing that one's life is in the hand of a loving God. He understands the trials and struggles. He is watching over His people. There may be times that one thinks that one can't take anymore. But the Lord, the silversmith is watching over His child.

Another interesting point about the smelting of silver is that the silver is placed in the hottest part of the flame. The silversmith will hold the silver in the blue flame. He keeps his eye on the silver until it is ready.

For me this is a very difficult time. It is difficult to be in the crucible and go through this time of purification. But it is there that I found myself. It is during that time that I reevaluated my life and what was happening. It was during that time that my focus needed to be on the one who was holding me and not the flame. When my focus was on the one who was holding me, I understood that this time had a purpose. It did not take the heat away, but I knew there was Someone that you could turn to.

Another thing I learned was that there are two ways that the silver-smith knows that the silver is ready. The first is that it starts to glow. The second way is that the silversmith sees his reflection. Both of these images are wonderful lessons.

There are certain faces that come to mind for me when I think about friends who have had a life of suffering, and their witness shone their love for their God. These precious servants of God encouraged me much more than I could ever encourage them. They understood that there was much hardship in their lives, but God's love for them was greater. They were lights of the goodness and faithfulness of God.

One of my favorite images is the second one where the silversmith sees his reflection in the smelting silver. These same people come to mind. They accepted it because they understood that God is good and these trials do not deny the goodness of God nor His love for them. I pray that during my time of trial people did not see somebody who was bitter, someone who was a victim, or someone who needed pity. I pray they saw a reflection of God, patient, loving, and forgiving.

Prayer — Dear Lord, thank You that You have my life in Your hands. Thank You that Your eye is upon me during the heat of the trial. You are attentive to me. Help me to not lose faith or confidence. Help others to see Your love through the glow of my life. Help others to see Your reflection in my words, actions, and attitudes. In Jesus' name, amen.

Scripture Readings for Day 28:

Isaiah 41

But you, Israel, my servant,
    Jacob, whom I have chosen,
    the offspring of Abraham, my friend;
you whom I took from the ends of the earth,
    and called from its farthest corners,
saying to you, "You are my servant,
    I have chosen you and not cast you off";
fear not, for I am with you;
    be not dismayed, for I am your God;
I will strengthen you, I will help you,
    I will uphold you with my righteous right hand.

I was with you all the time

I know that your life changed
The day I called your wife.
You went through all the motions
Just to get along through life.
You lost so much that day.
Life had no reason, no rhyme.
But I want to assure you this.
I was with you all the time.

I was there when I called her home.
I was there when you were all alone.
I was there in your friend's embrace.
I was there, wiped the tears from your face.
I was there. I was there.

Your home was once solace
Then quiet was not your friend.
The loneliness engulfed you.
The nights would never end.
Family helped you through it.
Friends, they were a sign.
I did not leave you by yourself.
I was with you all the time.

I was there when they came to call
I was there when you did fall.
I was there right by your side.
I was there each time you cried.
I was there. I was there.

I listened to your groaning.
I heard your cries and tears.
I walked right beside you.
I was there to calm your fears.
You felt you were abandoned.
Too much, it was a crime.
You were lost with no direction.
But I was with you all the time.

I was there with each friend who prayed.
I was there in the words they said.
I was there in the cards they wrote.
I was there and I did take note.
I was there. I was there.

Day 28

I was with you all the time
Isaiah 41:8-10

There are times that you think that not only has God abandoned you; He has also forgotten you. Although I tried to find comfort in the faithfulness of God, there were those days that I could not make any sense of why Jill died and I now had to be the sole parent to my son. Jill would be doing a much better job of this than I am, I thought.. After I returned to Michigan and my life started to unravel, I felt that way at times. I couldn't understand how I could feel the way that I did if God was with me. I believed that it was true, but what I felt and what I believed seemed to be in conflict.

I am so glad that God is greater and bigger than my feelings. The truth is God was there when my wife died. He was with her to direct her home to be with Him. God was with me and Marco to encourage us in the days after Jill's death. God made his presence known in the family of faith that surrounded us. He was with us through our family that traveled from Georgia and Michigan to be with us. God was with us through the faithful friends who brought food and words of encouragement. God was with us through the friends who prayed for us then and continue to pray for us today. God was with me through the friends who said an encouraging word or gave a hug at just the right moment, not knowing how much it meant. God was with me as I gathered with the saints in worship. God was with me when Marco and I did our evening devotions and prayed. God was with me as I read the Bible and prayed. God was with me when I lay in bed and couldn't sleep. God was with me when I cried out and asked Him where He was.

I know that God was with me because He promised to be there. Here are some of those promises that I held on to for strength:

Matthew 28:20 — I am with you always, to the end of the age.

John 14:18 — I will not leave you as orphans. I will come to you.

Joshua 1:9 — Be strong and be courageous. Do not be frightened and do not be dismayed, for the Lord your God is with you wherever you go.

Isaiah 41:10 —Fear not, for I am with you; do not be dismayed, for I am your God; I will strengthen you, I will help you; I will uphold you with my righteous right hand.

Isaiah 43:2 —When you pass through the waters I will be with you, and through the rivers, they shall not overcome you, when you walk through the fire, you will not be burned, the flame shall not consume you.

Isaiah 43:5 — Fear not, for I am with you. I will bring your offspring from the east, and from the west I will gather you.

God gave me these promises. He commits Himself to his word. He commits himself to me. I can trust in God and I can trust his promises.

Prayer — Dear Lord, sometimes I feel so alone. I feel that way but I know that it is not true. Don't let my feelings get in the way. Help me to not only trust Your promises but to believe they are the reality in my life. In Jesus' name, amen.

John 10

So Jesus again said to them, "Truly, truly, I say to you, I am the door of the sheep. ⁸ All who came before me are thieves and robbers, but the sheep did not listen to them. ⁹ I am the door. If anyone enters by me, he will be saved and will go in and out and find pasture. **The thief comes only to steal and kill and destroy. I came that they may have life and have it abundantly**. I am the good shepherd. The good shepherd lays down his life for the sheep. He who is a hired hand and not a shepherd, who does not own the sheep, sees the wolf coming and leaves the sheep and flees, and the wolf snatches them and scatters them. He flees because he is a hired hand and cares nothing for the sheep. I am the good shepherd. I know my own and my own know me, just as the Father knows me and I know the Father; and I lay down my life for the sheep. And I have other sheep that are not of this fold. I must bring them also, and they will listen to my voice. So there will be one flock, one shepherd. For this reason the Father loves me, because I lay down my life that I may take it up again. No one takes it from me, but I lay it down of my own accord. I have authority to lay it down, and I have authority to take it up again. This charge I have received from my Father."

That your life would be full

John 10:10

I've been struggling with the thieves and the robbers.
They've been walking in and out of my life.
They come in the dark to take my hope and comfort.
Then they replace it with so much strife.
Their goals are to distract and confuse me.
To focus on the pain and to forget the hope.
To make me think that each day will get worse.
At times they get the best of me, I can't cope.

Chorus
But a voice cries out in the darkness.
A voice that cuts like a knife.
I hear the voice of the shepherd.
I came that you might have life.
I came that your life would be full.
So much more than the life you're living.
A life of joy, of hope, and purpose.
That basks in the gifts I've given.

I've been talking to the thieves and robbers.
I've told them they're no longer welcome here.
I'm so done with their lies and deceptions.
I'm on to their tricks to cause me fear.
There's a much better way to be living.
It starts by list'ning to another voice.
I can't decide life's circumstances.
But how I respond? That is my choice.

Now I'm walking with the shepherd.
All that's changed is that you're by my side.
The loss and the hurt still scar my life.
But my joy will not be denied.
You've taken on these enemies
Who sought my life to destroy.
In place of all their deceptions,
You've fill my life with joy.

This voice cries out in the darkness,
A voice that cuts like a knife.
I hear the voice of the shepherd.
I came that you might have life.
I came that your life would be full.
A voice that tells of promises fulfilled.
A voice that assures the greatest love.
At long last, my sad heart is thrilled.

Day 29
That you might have life
John 10:10

The question that I have for you is this: Who have you let set up residence in your life? Whose voice or voices are you listening to? The voice that you listen to has an upper hand on how you are going to live your life. There are voices that want to sap you of all hope and joy. But there is a voice that not only wants you to have hope and joy, but it wants you to have a full life.

Too long I listened to the wrong voices. That is the wise way that Satan works. He wants to distance you from your source of life. As long as you listen to the wrong voices- doubt, fear, anger, hatred, self-pity, jealousy, self-deprecation, and failure, you are going to see yourself in that light.

These are the tools that the thieves and robbers use to rob you of life. They are very effective tools. The good news is that they tools are easily defended against and made useless. The first step is to recognize that these voices are ones that you should not be giving the time of day. They have as their goal separating you from God. They want to distract you so that you lose focus of what God has done for you and that He is with you. The second step is to recognize that Satan is the one who is giving them a voice. His goal is to separate you from God. It worked for Adam and Eve. He has a tried and true method to make you sin and lead you away from God. He makes you question if God really wants what best for you. Next, he drives a wedge between God and you because I can't trust what God says. Then he offers a "better" way because God wants to keep us down. Too many times you bite. I know I do.

But there's a Shepherd. His voice is always calling out to His sheep. How wonderful it is when our ears are attuned to His voice. Our shepherd wants only what is best for us. Our Shepherd wants us to not only listen to His voice but also that we follow Him. As we follow, He promises certain things along the way. "I will keep you safe. I know there are dangers. There are robbers and thieves. There are predators along the way." The Shepherd does more than promise to put Himself between us and them. Our Shepherd laid down His life for you and me and took it up again. The robbers, the thieves, and the predators know what He has done and they know that they can only do harm when we get separated from the shepherd. Our shepherd is leading us to the green pastures. He's leading us to the still waters. He's leading us through the valleys to the secure places that He has prepared. There are those precious times in our life when I am complete joy. I know that I am in the presence of God and all is right. There are those times when I am at complete peace. The promises of God are my reality. I feel like I am sitting in the Lord's lap. Nothing is being said; nothing needs to be said. There is no doubt. God loves me, and He's with me. There are those precious times when I not only know that God loves me but I experience that love. That is the fullness of life that Jesus is talking about. That is why Jesus came into our lives. That is what God has in store for us, not just for a time but for eternity.

Prayer — O Lord, too long I listened to the robbers and the thieves. Too long, I was frightened by the predators. Let me listen to Your voice alone. As I follow You, lead me so that I understand that You have come so that I realize the fullness of life that You promised through Jesus. In His name, amen.

Scripture Readings for Day 30:

Isaiah 43

But now thus says the LORD,
he who created you, O Jacob,
    he who formed you, O Israel:
"Fear not, for I have redeemed you;
    I have called you by name, you are mine.
When you pass through the waters, I will be with you;
    and through the rivers, they shall not overwhelm you;
when you walk through fire you shall not be burned,
    and the flame shall not consume you.
For I am the LORD your God,
    the Holy One of Israel, your Savior.
I give Egypt as your ransom,
    Cush and Seba in exchange for you.
Because you are precious in my eyes,
    and honored, and I love you,
I give men in return for you,
    peoples in exchange for your life.
Fear not, for I am with you;
    I will bring your offspring from the east,
    and from the west I will gather you.
I will say to the north, Give up,
    and to the south, Do not withhold;
bring my sons from afar
    and my daughters from the end of the earth,
everyone who is called by my name,
    whom I created for my glory,
    whom I formed and made."

You Were with Me through the Fire

Isaiah 43:2

My life was burning down
As I ran around that night.
With no smile and no movement
She was taken from my sight.
We sped off to the hospital.
Things would never be the same.
The whys and guilt ran through my mind
Racing between guilt and pain.

Chorus
You were with me through the fire.
My life came crashing down.
You were my one confidence
As my life burned to the ground
Hope and dreams went up in flames
When You called her to Your side.
Just living in the ashes
Waiting for heartache to subside.

Walking through the aftermath
Feeling numb from all the loss.
Stumbling through the rubble
Unaware how great the cost.
I know my life is different.
I can never go back home.
I'll never hear her voice again.
I pray Your Kingdom come.

But You're with me through the fire.
Though there's destruction all around.
And only losses can be found.
You have me in Your arm,
Protecting me from harm.
Yes, You're with me through the fire.
When all is said and done I know,
You were with me through the fire.

Day 30
With Me Through the Fire
Isaiah 43:1-7

Fire has a devastating power. All it does is consume and leave destruction. Those who have lost their house through fire feel helpless as the fire destroys all that they worked for, all their memories, and many of the things that they hold dear. For those who have walked through the remains of a forest fire, there is an eerie or macabre feeling that comes over them. This is the place where animals lived and flourished. This is where one could walk and feel peace. Now it seems surreal. There should be life, but there is death. There should be the whistling of the wind, the songs of the birds, and the bustle of the squirrels. All is silent. Fire destroys.

Death does the same thing. After Jill died, I did not want to be in the house by myself. My home and quiet were my enemies. Together we searched for that house. We worked on it to make it a home. Nearly seven years we lived there together. Five of those years were with a child who came when he was nine months until he was nearly six. This was our haven. But she died in the bedroom, in my arms. I did not want to sleep in that room for months. I would walk through the room on the way to the closet and the bathroom. But I avoided it. The backyard was our respite. Marco would play in the pool while Jill and I sipped our margaritas. It went abandoned. I would take Marco someplace else to play in the water. Death had destroyed our happy home.

But there was a family that survived. Marco and I remained. More importantly, is that God was with us as well. He promised to be there. At first, that was all that we had to make sense of Jill's death. I have no idea how many times I said to Marco, "Mommy's brain broke. The doctors couldn't help her. She's with Jesus now." We couldn't make any sense of what was happening. The fire known as death had done its work in our lives.

But Jesus was there. That promise of Mommy being with Jesus brought us comfort. I wish I would have held on to the second part of the promise just as strongly. God was with us. The second part of the promise is "when you walk through fire you will not be burned" (Isaiah 43:2). He was with me as He reminded me of all His promises. Countless times I said to myself. "I am the resurrection and the life, he who believes in me will live; though he die, yet shall he live." I believed this promise for Jill because her trust was in the Lord. I found great comfort in the promise of Revelation, "He will wipe every tear from their eyes, and death shall be no more" (Revelation 21:2). God was with me through the family of faith that walked with me, encouraging me through the loss with compassion. God was with me with Marco. I don't know how I would have survived if it wasn't for him. He helped give me a reason to get up in the morning and to continue going forward. I wanted to honor Jill through him.

After a house burns down or a forest is destroyed, a new life begins. A house is rebuilt. The forest begins to grow again. Life goes on. Jill has moved on and is with our Lord. Marco and I have to make sense of this new life together. God is still with us. God is still in control. God has not left us by ourselves.

I hope you can apply these promises to your life as well. There are times that all you see is the destruction. There are times that you feel like your life has been destroyed. Trust this promise. God is with you. God will not leave you by yourself. You may not feel His presence. You may not experience joy or peace, but that does not deny God's presence. Remember this precious promise of God- nothing can separate you from God. For I am sure that neither life nor death, nor angels nor rulers, nor things present nor things to come, nor powers, nor height nor depth, nor anything else in all creation can separate me from the love of God in Christ Jesus, our Lord (Romans 8:38, 39).

Prayer — O Lord, sometimes all I see is the death and the destruction. Help me to see that You are with me. You were with me through each step of this grief journey. There are times that I have lost sight of you. You have never lost sight of me nor removed from me your arm of protection. Help me remember and find strength and encouragement in You and Your presence, in Jesus' name. Amen

Scripture Readings for Day 31:

Isaiah 40

Have you not known? Have you not heard?
The LORD is the everlasting God,
　　the Creator of the ends of the earth.
He does not faint or grow weary;
　　his understanding is unsearchable.
^{29} He gives power to the faint,
　　and to him who has no might he increases strength.
^{30} Even youths shall faint and be weary,
　　and young men shall fall exhausted;
^{31} but they who wait for the LORD shall renew their strength;
　　they shall mount up with wings like eagles;
they shall run and not be weary;
　　they shall walk and not faint.

You Lift Me Up

Isaiah 40:31

The path I'm on's a struggle.
And there is no end in sight.
Each mile brings a new trial.
I'm ready to give up the fight.

But you lift me up.
You give me strength along the way.
You fill my cup.
To renew my soul to face the day.

Now all I see are battles.
The enemy's all around.
He strikes where I am weakest.
Now my face is to the ground.

But you lift me up.
You put me on your wings.
And you fill my cup.
I see you and I start to sing.

Oh, how can I continue
When my rival will not stop?
He knows where I am weakest.
And he won't cease until I drop.

But you lift me up.
You give me strength with each step I take.
And you fill my cup.
My will to thrive will never break.

Day 31
You Lift Me Up
Isaiah 40:31

The promise that God gives you is that it is worth the wait. When I was growing up, there was a catsup commercial. It had people getting frustrated as they waited for the catsup to finally come out of the bottle. While they were waiting, the song "Anticipation" played in the background. The idea was it was worth the wait because of what was inside that bottle.

I have been in a battle. This battle has been going on a long time; in fact, it has been going on too long. During the whole time, I trusted in the promises of God. I held on to the faithfulness of the One who made those promises. I held to those promises because throughout Scripture, God demonstrated Himself to be faithful. I held on to the promises because God has proven Himself to be faithful in my life.

There was a long time that nothing was happening in my life to justify that trust in God. My life was not getting better. In fact, it was going in the opposite direction. One of the promises that God made that I held on to was that "he who began a good work in me would bring it to completion" (Philippians 1:6). I know that God called me to be a child of God. He also called me as a pastor to serve as an under shepherd for the sheep He has called. God does not want my story to end in failure. God does not want to leave me broken. This was the season that I needed to be comforted and encouraged: so that I would be prepared to bring that comfort to others. I believed this would happen. I just did not know when or how.

Another promise I held on to was Romans 8:28. "We know that for those who love God all things work together for the good of those who are called according to his purpose". I did want to try to get into the mind of God to try to understand why Jill had to die. Maybe because I knew that it wouldn't help because Jill would not be with us anyway. But I trusted that when I came out of the grief and the hurt,

God would use that so that I could be a blessing to others. I pray that this book is a part of that promise being fulfilled.

Another verse that encouraged me was Isaiah 40:31: "But they who wait for the LORD shall renew their strength; they shall mount up with wings like eagles; they shall run and not be weary; they shall walk and not faint." I love the imagery of being on the wings of an eagle. I have hiked when I had no strength at all. The thought of soaring effort-lessly while having the most incredible view is incredible. Going from plodding along, trying to get out of the canyon, to somebody else doing all the work and going faster than you can imagine with a view that you thought you never would have, is overwhelming. There were times that I was just holding on, barely holding on at that. I have not started to soar yet. But I am not sapped of energy either. I am definitely not thinking about throwing in the towel. But God is renewing my strength. I am certain of not just the promise of God's presence, but the blessing of God's presence. I'll never be the person I was before. In my youth, I was a source of joy. That's all I knew so that is what I had to share. God has made me a different and stronger person. I can now help those who are grieving with the authenticity of my story. The promises of God are the same. But I am one who was weary, and the Lord has renewed my strength.

Prayer — O Lord, You are my strength. You come to me when I am weary. You recognize my weakened state. You lift me up with Your word of promise and your presence. You fill my cup with Your Spirit and the assurance that You have not forgotten me or forsaken me. In Jesus' name, amen.

Alternate Songs

Author's note:
I wrote a couple of duplicate songs and here they are.

Day 26

I'm gonna pray through this

This house was once filled with laughter.
A smile welcomed me at the break of day.
Oh, my love, and my companion,
With no warning was taken away.
My life now has no direction
I'm trying to make sense of it all
My emptiness soon takes over me.
So to my knees I need to fall

Chorus
I'm gonna pray through this.
I'm holding on to the one who has a hold on me.
I'm gonna pray through this.
I'm looking to the one who is looking after me.
I'm gonna pray through this.
I'm coming to the one who came for me.
I'm gonna pray through this.
I'm trusting the promises of the one who promises.

I don't know how this has happened.
How I ever came to this place.
I look at myself in the mirror.
I don't recognize that face.
Once carefree and full of life
Now an empty stare in the eyes.
Who is that person that I see there?
Someone fallen no more to rise?

The night brings no consolation.
My mind starts running wild.
The sheep are running rampant.
Shaking like a frightened child.
Nothing I do seems to help.
There are no dreams for me.
Waiting for the first light of day
Hoping to change this story.

Day 30

He's with me through the fire

Isaiah 43:2

The flames are blazing.
The fire is cracking.
Ashes fill the air.
The heat is scorching.
The smoke, it billows.
There's chaos everywhere.

Chorus
But he's with me through the fire.
Though there's destruction all around.
And only losses can be found.
He has me in His arm,
Protecting me from harm.
Yes, He's with me through the fire.

Ev'rything is charred.
The ashes smolder.
The fire has done its worst.
The smoke, it lingers.
How the tears abound.
Feeling lost and so cursed.

I've been through the fire as my life burned down.
When what was secure crashed to the ground.
The one who walked by my side
With whom I laughed and I cried.
Was taken too soon, O Lord, what to do?
Living in the remnants of what is left.
Trying to survive and do what is best.
What is left? Or what is right?
Lord, get me through this endless night!
Lord, I will never make it without You.
He rushes into the fire
He wraps me in his arms.
He covers my face.
He takes me from the fire
He helps me breathe.
And from his cup I drink.
Now safe from the fire.

When all is said and done I know,
He was with me through the fire

Psalms from the Pit

Psalm 28

To you, O Lord, I call; my rock, be not deaf to me,
    lest, if you be silent to me,
    I become like those who go down to the pit.
Hear the voice of my pleas for mercy, when I cry to you for help,
    when I lift up my hands toward your most holy sanctuary.

Psalm 30:

I will extol you, O Lord, for you have drawn me up
    and have not let my foes rejoice over me.
O Lord my God, I cried to you for help,
    and you have healed me.
O Lord, you have brought up my soul from Sheol;
    you restored me to life
    from among those who go down to the pit.

Psalm 40:

I waited patiently for the Lord;
    he inclined to me and heard my cry.
He drew me up from the pit of destruction, out of the miry bog,
    and set my feet upon a rock, making my steps secure.
He put a new song in my mouth, a song of praise to our God.
    Many will see and fear, and put their trust in the Lord.

Psalm 88:

For my soul is full of troubles,
    and my life draws near to Sheol.
I am counted among those who go down to the pit;
    I am a man who has no strength,
like one set loose among the dead,
    like the slain that lie in the grave,
like those whom you remember no more,
    for they are cut off from your hand.
You have put me in the depths of the pit,
    in the regions dark and deep.
Your wrath lies heavy upon me,
    and you overwhelm me with all your waves. Selah

Psalm 143:

Answer me quickly, O Lord! My spirit fails!
    Hide not your face from me,
    lest I be like those who go down to the pit.
Let me hear in the morning of your steadfast love,
    for in you I trust.
Make me know the way I should go, for to you I lift up my soul.